Thomas J Jenkins

Six Seasons on our Prairies and Six Weeks in our Rockies

Thomas J Jenkins

Six Seasons on our Prairies and Six Weeks in our Rockies

ISBN/EAN: 9783744693288

Printed in Europe, USA, Canada, Australia, Japan

Cover: Foto ©Thomas Meinert / pixelio.de

More available books at **www.hansebooks.com**

SIX SEASONS

ON OUR PRAIRIES

AND

SIX WEEKS IN OUR ROCKIES.

BY

THOMAS J. JENKINS

OF THE DIOCESE OF LOUISVILLE.

PUBLISHED BY

CHAS. A. ROGERS.

167 WEST JEFFERSON STREET, LOUISVILLE, KY.

1884.

Knœfel, Berne & Co., Printers,
210 Market St., Louisville, Ky.

TO THE

EVER-VIRGIN QUEEN MARY,

Immaculate and **First** Patroness of these States, whose Dower is the

WHOLE NEW WORLD,

And by Excellence, the Best it Contains in the

NORTHERN PRAIRIE VALLEY,

Watered by **her own** "**River** of the IMMACULATE CONCEPTION,"

And Bounded, towards the Setting Sun, by **the**

WALLS OF OUR ROCKY MOUNTAINS,

Inlaid with **Gold, Silver,** and Precious Stones,

Emblematic all of what we would offer

OUR ONLY QUEEN,

This Slight Attempt to Mirror Forth

HER VIRGIN LANDS, is Dedi-

cated, **with all the** Effusion

of his Heart **and** with all

the Ardor of his Inmost

Soul, by her forever

DEVOTED CLIENT,

THE AUTHOR.

May,

1884.

SIX SEASONS ON OUR PRAIRIES:

A DIARY.

SIX SEASONS ON OUR PRAIRIES.

A PREFATORY MAY.

IT WAS on the first of May, in the year of grace 1882, we three—a practical Irish Kentucky farmer, his sturdy son, a young man of good, hard sense, and an ailing ecclesiastic—started to travel **North** and West by the circuitous but interesting route, across Southern Indiana and Illinois, and from St. Louis **by** water to the other saintly city in Minnesota. We went sight-seeing and health-seeking, as well as on business intent, to secure personal knowledge of prairie farming, **by** "doing" the Northwestern Catholic Colonies—with possible and probable choice of new homes for some families who **were** wearing out both patience and good Irish **and** American muscle on Middle-Kentucky farms lying back from the Ohio, and cut off from railroad lines. The agitation for the migration of Catholics from the crowded cities East, and the poorer agricultural districts South, was inaugurated fourteen or fifteen years ago. The plan was carried into execution beyond the Mississippi River, so that we find a more or less connected system of plantings scattered in every State bordering its western banks. Practical **laymen have joined** hands with practical prelates all

along the line, and Catholics find themselves provided with resources to place families with moderate
means, and no good establishment where they live
or come from, to people the glorious West, and
take possession of their God-given inheritance.
Deus fac sit! For ourselves, we did not get off
without some difficulty. Embarking rather late in
the day we boarded the wrong boat on the Ohio to
make rail connections on the other shore. Here
we were separated by some misunderstanding—two
of us finally bunking on the floor of the state-room-
less craft all night, as it made its regular or rather
irregular trips. Mishap No. 1. Mishap No. 2 follows on its heels. We united next morning, and
moved on towards St. Louis—to be caught on the
way by a furious hail-storm, that made the car-top
and windows rattle like musketry, as we neared the
big city of the Father of Waters. The place, strange
to us, we booked in the Planter House—imposing
enough when you were inside the colonnaded office.
We were shown to a room with three beds, the
lights smashed by the hail, and scattered glass and
ice all over the floor. When we came to pay our
bill, and the clerk coolly informed us it was nine
dollars for a night's lodging alone, we looked from
one to the other in amazement, but after demurring,
paid him the outrageous charge. He didn't know
par. example, that one of the costliest boats on the
Ohio—the unfortunate "Pat. Cleburne"—had been
blown up for charging one of us somewhere about
eight or nine dollars too much for carriage. He was
innocent—that Planter House clerk. It was not two,
at most three, months afterwards, when the Planter

concern was burned to the ground, with a great loss, uninsured. And we assure the suspicious that we caused neither catastrophe, but considered both as providential retribution, sure to overtake those persisting in legalizable theft.

May the 9th, and we had steamed up the ever more beautiful **Northern** Mississippi, noting particularly the thriftier towns and cities on the Western prairie side, the fresher air, the limpider water, the painted rocks, and realizing how poetic and true was the Catholic instinct that named this upper continental stream the "Immaculate Conception." Hail, spirits of heroic priests and men! We other Catholic wayfarers salute you with reverential love as we pass.

Our tarry in and about St. Paul was short. We had come for everything but big cities and grand buildings. We moved westward.

I will admonish the reader that tho' the writer was, the whole three seasons in the prosperous year of 1882, traveling on the prairies, as well as during the corresponding time of which a diary follows in 1883, no detailed account of the first half of these six seasons was kept. The account of one set of seasons will answer for the other, and 1882 will be noticed only supplementarily, and as occasions recall it, except the relation of this month of May.

We found it cool—cold to our Southern blood; and woe to him who had come unprovided with his overcoat—as one of us had! It was a constant source of fun for us two, and occasional shivering and self-reproach to him.

Taking the Northwestern route from St. Paul on

the way to Graceville, Minn., on the borders of Middle Dakota, we were not favorably impressed with the wisdom of the projectors of the way towns. Following the railroad strictly many of the villages and more pretentious places were built in sloughy situations, and had to have their streets mounded to keep somewhat out of the water.

Much of the country contiguous to the older Catholic foundations of colonies, in Swift and adjoining counties at, for instance, Waverly, De Graff, Clontarf, and further north, on examination, proved to be generally good, if well selected; though tracts are found more or less marshy. Sections can be picked, which, with drainage by ditching or tiling, make good farms and fine crops. Some such I already saw in tillage, and of fine records. It is considerably similar to Northern Illinois, some ninety or one hundred miles south of Chicago. New selections have been made at Adrian, Minneota, and southward.

To Minneota, Rev. Fr. Cornelis, the former pastor, has just brought from his native land one hundred new families of Belgians, mostly farmers. So successful in their own garden country of Europe, they are sure to succeed on these prairies.

Graceville—named after the present venerable second Bishop of St. Paul—Rt. Rev. Thomas L. Grace, O. P. D. D.—is a rising town, and surrounded by perhaps a better country than is met east or southeast in Minnesota. Communities of this kind are left to their own resources, and are not "boomed" like numerous localities—in fact, the whole of the region west. It has attracted, however, some two hundred families in a moderate radius; and the vil-

lage boasts of goodly rows of houses, a large mill
and general stores. There is a belt of natural timber
three-quarters of a mile from town, of large trees of
various kinds—a resource for firewood not often
attainable on the prairie from the Dakota line, as far
east and south as Swift County, Minn. Outside
the great pineries of the North, which cover, with
other wooded portions, one-third of the area of the
State; and the "Big Woods" of some thirty varieties
of timber, and containing, in its breadth of forty
miles, and length of upwards of one hundred, 5,000
square miles, wood is scarce, except about the
larger lakes.

Spring ploughing and planting were going on
actively in the middle of May here and in Southwestern Minnesota; tho' as shall be remarked, there
is a difference of from fifteen to twenty days in the
maturing, as in the earlier planting, of crops as compared with the wooded regions in Southeastern
Minnesota.

Of game there was all abundance. We kept our
table well supplied with plover, jack-rabbits, snipe
and other varieties of smaller game. We chased a
rabbit one day, looking fully as large as an ordinary
dog, but caught—only a good glimpse of him, notably his uplifted cotton tail.

Towards the middle of the month we shifted our
headquarters to Avoca, Minn., and came into the
charming region detailfully described, in all its
moods and phases, in the Diary of 1883.

This Diary embodies my diurnal and nocturnal
experiences, not only, tho' mainly, in the "Land of
Sky-tinted Waters," but also excursions into Iowa,

West and East; Dakota; Nebraska thro' its whole
length; Wyoming's southern corner; the "Rockies"
in Colorado.   It does not forget general items of
Catholic, mineral and agricultural interests in Montana, Idaho, Nevada, New Mexico; and winds up
with comparisons of the States lying on both sides
of the Mississippi Valley.

If descriptions seem to crowd the early months
and the latest, the reader will be the more astonished
that Nature is so various and interesting on what are
esteemed as flat, dull, prairie lands.   And Nature's,
because God's remedies, are prescribed for ills of mind
and body.   The Diary's range precludes the idea
of its being classed with what I at least ignore—
special booming campaign papers; does not, however, disdain to tell all the inviting truth it can lay
hold on, and where proper, give details worth knowing to projecting movers, to enable them to judge
for themselves when they come to examine localities
for future homes.   Finally, I believe and confess,
with Mr. John Sweetman, the experienced and candid author of "Recent Experiences in the Colonization of Irish Families," that it is as well—nay just—
to show some of both sides of the practical settling
of Catholic or other families on our Western
prairies.   A man and a priest need not stick at
acknowledging a few palpable disadvantages, and
predicting the certain disappointments of too gold-
en dreamers.   "Forewarned is forearmed"—still the
good will prevail, like Truth—and here is proof of it.

DIARY OF THE SEASONS OF 1883.

AVOCA, MINNESOTA, June 6th, 1883.

WHY not? It can be vain—it's useful, and, one day, interesting. And to store up facts and observations for a future period! My friends, too, how sweet for them! Then on, Auspice Maria! Let's mirror the Virgin Lands. City Diaries? What? Musty, dusty, great cities. Away with the necessary evils! Now for the necessary good. Walls are manufactured—towns built by men—God made the fields and "their beauty is with him." They are temples "made without hands"—God-made. The best is not the rare—contrariwise. The best beautiful is cheap, common for all. Men! make but a pond in imitation of that Lake St. Rose. Paint but a feather in semblance of this poor bird's that clings to my fingers from the hunt. The undefiled—alas! except it all be sin-tainted—is here over the ocean of the prairie, in the changeful face of the waters and the sky. I repeat: "God made the country—man made the town:" or, as some will have it, it was the old enemy made the town.

Just two weeks to-day! Ah! what a long day since I came. Night has at last been dissolving under the influence of this pure air of heaven, the balmy breezes, the sweet sunshine. I have begun .to sleep. "Ho!" said the housekeeper, "father, it's

after seven by this clock." I was conscious enough to
respond: "Oh! your clock is too fast." I feel sleepy
in the day, after my hearty meals. After-dinner
nap—I'm afraid, bah! I'm not afraid either, why not
be glad?—will be the order of commencing the
evening properly. Repose, I have lost plenty!
aye, superabundance, and I'm going to make it up
this summer, please God. Besides, the days are so
long—just think, from 4.22 to 7.38, fifteen hours,
sixteen minutes; nay, over seventeen hours of daylight, including the two hours' twilight. The half
moon hangs out her silver lamp and the stars fade.

June 15*th*.—That was a prefatial plea in advance
for a longer sleep this morning; ahem! arose at
7 o'clock whistle. Let's put it on the storm and the
pup that pawed the door open. I heard him leisurely scratching himself beside my couch at something near 4 A. M., and drove him out with my
boot.

Moore might extenuate, paraphrastically:

> "The best of all ways to shorten long days,
> Is to lengthen the hours of the night."

M. W. Spring, of the University of Liege's, Popular Science Monthly article, "On the Colors of
Water," might be illustrated in the lakes of this region, notably St. Rose's. Its face changes like the
human physiognomy—all depends upon its mood.
When very angry or placidly calm, its color is dark
blue, almost purple. In medium, undecided weather,
its cast is more inclined to earthy, a brownish red.
But curious to say, when the main body is reddish,
the slough beyond the railroad bridge and mound
appears deep, beautiful blue. I will watch this,

The sky influences as much as the lake bottom, and the season again makes remarkable differences. The water now appears *in se*, of a light brownish tinge, except on the pebbles.

WHITE BEAR LAKE, MINNESOTA.

June 15th.—Curious, how this rainy, falling day should make sunshine within and bring me back those unparalleled days of first delighted experience in this crystal climate—when it wants to be crystal. White Bear Lake, twelve miles east of St. Paul, commands some eighteen miles of shore and is diversified by not only the now smooth, now ascending banks on inlet and bay; but far off to the northern end is dignified with a promontory of uncommon beauty and pleasant surprise. Across the causeway, too, is a secluded offing where grow the yellow and white waterlily, the former rather indelicate, but the latter approaching the exquisiteness of the night-blooming Cereus. We would stoop and reach down low into the water to catch the stem long, and detach it from its vase-like socket. These and wild roses, meadow sweet, larkspurs, and baybells mingled their sweets about our Lady's feet in the May services. How many and varied in form, hue and scent, the wild flowers on the shores about the green avenues of the oft-rifled island: Sweet Williams, wild violets and saffron blossoms, calla lilies, and purple bunches of fragrant lilacs. And how vivifying the bevies of joyous youths and maidens in their gay summer costumes, culling them and sporting in the checkered shades by the beach and bluffy outlooks on the occassional stretches of lake.

When I look back now to last summer, at the perfect days and heavenly nights at "White Bear,"
domesticated as I was with the cultivated family
who made my stay so pleasant, I marvel how I
could not sleep. I was unstrung indeed. A man
may laugh at nerves before he discovers he has any;
but let him hang over the ragged edge of suppressed
or excited palpitation for a run of twelve or fifteen
nights without the break of a solid rest for even four
hours! And, well—I used to sit in the spring sunlight,
which makes diamonds on the lake, opals in the sky,
and emeralds and amethysts on the leaves of the
wooded shores, and see as distinctly as a crystal in a
microscope the exact form of the remotest objects
sharply defined. The large island, with winding
drives, piled tiers of shaggy trees and lake-lapped,
was being connected to the main land by an arching,
balustraded bridge. The shores, down by the music
balcony and on to Williams' Hotel, were dotted on
land by the peeping tents and white villas, and
spacious retired hotels; while bobbing near the
shores, the sailcraft invited you to a scud across the
bays or out into the deep. The green and red bath
houses and out-jutting piers formed accompanying
ground and background for the lounging fishers,
flapping sails and pleasure hunters. Our moon-lit
nights out in our swift sailers, with violin and flag-
eolet or flute, according with the lightsome boat-
songs or opera snatches, kept young hearts sweet
and fresh, raised the drooping, rejuvenated the older,
smoothed the wrinkles of care.

The inhabitants about White Bear, when the
weather is stormy, and the blue waves trembling

out in mid-lake, dash up a crest of white foam, say: "The Bear is showing his teeth!" How beautiful! White Bear, tho', you are aware, is the Indian chief's name, who is buried in the fine mound with the rustic arbor, made in vacation by an ecclesiastical student, but naturally utilized by lounging lovers as midway station in their round of the lake shore.

Avoca, June 15*th, night.*—How wonderfully various have been the past three or four days' sunsets across the lake. Monday's was an entrancing vision, more like the stories of Aladdin's Lamp or Mirza's vision—if not even recalling the Revelations of St. John. What a scene of ecstatic glory, calmly sublime! Bars of vivid lightning arrested in mid-volley, spread horizontally across the molten islands of liquid amber and onyx. The rounded, softer contours of the southwest and north gently burned like heaven's cornelians of rich red islands of clouded pearl, hillocks of feathery orange, filled out the back and upper ground. Away off to the horizon's south and north dwelt that indescribable peace of suffused pink light. About the sun there seemed a living, glorious tabernacle of white and rose and gold and precious metals burnished—a long island lay spread out of silvered gold "like purest glass." "He hath set in them a tabernacle for the sun," (*David Ps.*) and in the midst blazed with bearable effulgence the image of the Great King on his great white throne, diffusing glory and benediction for evermore. I gazed and was never sated with gazing, as the heavenly slides shifted the changing revelation, and an inspiration struck me to climb the highest point accessible over the lake and see

the mirrored glory in its fair bosom. I saw, and the
roses bloomed softly confused in the waters' depths,
a dream of a vision spread beneath, while the glory
above canopied all.

John Ruskin's great attraction was the grand-
iose—mountains, piled clouds, rushing torrents,
fiery glaciers. I have failed to notice that he has
any practical idea of plain beauty, simplicity, pastoral picturesqueness alone. Still and all, if he
had had opportunity to enjoy such a land as this,
such sky, such water, such air, the very names,
Minnetonka, "great waters" — Minnesota, "sky-
tinted waters," would have charmed him. He
missed something in all his wanderings through
Europe, Asia, even across the Mediterranean. He
never saw America, and say what they will, we certainly have the most superb natural scenery, without prescinding from the sublime, at least, in high
altitudes, the world can show. And one must travel
far before he will find any parallel with the unique
enchantment of these western prairies, when an eye
for the simple works of Nature, the attention to
details, the broadest and minutest, are appreciated.
This land, and its low-voiced, unobtrusive charm,
puts me in mind of the simple majesty of the word
of God, whose very most attractive feature is its
adaptability generally to all minds and all peoples
and times; which wears well and improves with
meditation, and palls not on long acquaintance.
Ruskin's truly æsthetic interpretation of the passages
from Holy Writ, describing the clouds as indeed
God's Throne and best manifestation of Himself in
Nature, came home, and a lofty peace awed my

awakened soul. Ezechiel: "Behold, He cometh with clouds and every eye shall see Him." Psalms: "Thy Mercy, O Lord, is in the heavens, and Thy faithfulness reacheth unto the clouds. His excellency is upon Israel and His strength is in the clouds." "The heavens declare His righteousness and all the people His glory." "Swear not by heaven, it is God's throne."

Tuesday's sunset was less beautiful—only orange and rose confused in sweet disorder, and about the north, colder heaps of creamy snow. Again, in the east, the slate-colored, elongated islands of solid vapor in a sea of greenish blue, and a grand tumbling of wrung-out rain clouds crowding the tops and sides of the vault. Wednesday's, finally, without a cloud; no side scenery, no varied colors, but one wide bosom of warm, red-rose light, forming an expansible hemisphere of comforting glory—spreading over the broad prairie and up into the western sky; the gold burning ball majestically sinking, sinking until the quarter disk, the centre of the half-periphery of heaven's Bengal light, seemed to draw, nay, did draw, the heart after it to witness the essential glory of which it was but the outward gate.

June 16th.—Yesterday's and this evening's train, bless it! brought my first batches of letters. My friends, that God has given me on occasions unlooked-for, but determined in his loving Providence, these are your self-drawn photographs, more precious

than the very artists', because drawn in the colors of
the heart. Here more than all does one begin to
appreciate them, the dear absent. How I have col-
lected them more carefully and culled them out with
greater solicitude than any other belonging.

Friends of mine in every clime, from the village
friends of first school days, when we coasted together
the great maple-tree hill-sides and waded the pure
rock-bound brook, on thro' school and seminary; in
Europe at our dear American College, and all thro'
these near fourteen years of joy-and-sorrow-check-
ered man's life, friends of unforgotten boyhood;
clinging hearts of young manhood; brothers-in-arms
in celestial warfare; sisters more of spirit than flesh,
sweetest because nearest my heart in God; children-
friends, to you all, living on earth, blessed in heaven,
I consecrate this page, only written, but indelible!
Orate pro me!

And here they troop to say their little speeches
before friendship's throne. How kindly my majesty
inclines towards them and gives a right royally gra-
cious hearing. "Ah! bléss you all, right well! Now
the 'winter of my discontent, doth thaw quite out in
the glow of your spring-time faces! Sweet friends,
glad welcome!"

And little by little, one comes down, like Joseph,
from his stateliness and mingles with his brothers
and sisters—and falling on their necks he weeps for
joy: "I am Joseph, come nearer to me—I am Joseph,
your brother."

Here is many a Benjamin and royal Judah, generous Reuben—aye, sometimes, repentant Issachar
and Zabulon. They will, many a time as now,

brighten my not unpleasant exile and freshen ties
never broken. All this gilded climate, new-found
friends, healthful benefits, would scarce fill the place
of a tithing of my loved correspondents, from the
gray-haired brethren in the ministry and sisters
under the white hood, to the children, known from
peachen-cheeked girlhood to the age of the
mother-eye and the purer cap of the religious.
Again, bless you all well and forever!

PRAIRIE SUNDAY.

Sunday, 17*th.*—The week is so quiet and Sabbath-
like out on these unpolluted prairies, and the stillness
of the Sunday is not striking, save for the ghost of
a holier calm that everywhere is its natural halo.
Only the little train, gliding almost noiselessly on
the level track, comes not back and forth; and the
single piping whistle of the tow-mill, playing tenor
to the bass of the droning machinery, is hushed.
But every day here is nearer like the day of the
Lord's rest than the busy, rushing, city church-going
and coming, the rattle of the street cars, and screech
and yell of the locomotives, and the jangling of the
different-voiced bells of the discordant creeds.

Avoca, Sunday Forenoon.—Some other friends
met me on the morning ramble along the lake in the
much-clouded sunshine that gave the moving,
glassy surface of St. Rose's the tint of watered blood.
Who would you guess? One would little expect a
sportsman—especially only an amateur and mediocre
"shot," to be a friend of the birds, eh! When such
cannot get legitimate game, they are apt to shoot for
fun and slay right and left, what they happen to hit.
Not so, however. One can love sport, not for the

sake of slaying, but to obtain necessary exercise,
irreplacable by anything different; to eke out the
scantier board, and because the fish of the waters
and birds of the air, as well as the beasts of the field,
are God-given for food, since the vegetarian diet
was abolished after the flood in the permission
accorded divinely to our second father. Familiar
friends! The cat-bird, with not only his short melo-
dious calls and fitful phrases, but his flat, soft cat-
call unmistakable. One struck up his intercalated
matins for, no doubt, the twentieth, or even fiftieth
repetition, down at the head of the lake near the
windmill; and as I sauntered up meditatively along
the shore to the west, I heard his notes sounding
clear over the half-caw of the multifarious varieties
of the black-birds, the clang-like notes of the prairie
lark, the whistle of the hovering plover and the
minor pipes of the winged mites, chirping, twitter-
ing along the bushes.

For a quarter of a mile or more, the pleasant notes
came borne by a gusting breeze, even sometimes
piercing past an adverse wind; and I could fairly
fancy myself in the wooded hills and sweeping vales
of old Kentucky. The illusion was eked out by the
frequent passing to and fro of the fan-tailed, fluttering beemartins; the distant, then nearer, short melody
of the clearer-throated lark, and the first fitful, then
swimming, flight of the tawny-breasted black-and-
yellow bird. Anon, as I lost the last notes of the
first songster, another set up his music box in the
bosk of the next lake-jutting, and took upwhere his
fellow-singer had left off.

Curious! the matins of the prairie birds continue
far into the day by reason of the uninterrupted

freshness of the mornings. Here, as the half-past-ten church bell calls to last Holy Mass, they chirp and chatter, call and quawk, sing singular melodies, and the irrepressible cock crows between.

17th—Still Sunday.—It has been fuller of incidents than usual. I got home from up the lake at 11:20 P. M. Up, then up and down the rapid little shoots of the inlet stream, around the graceful curves in the offings, we glided and threw out the troll hooks, spinning in the wake of the boat!

Houp, first bite! haul in: small pickerel. Second, a larger, still another, a half, a whole dozen, in something over an hour. The sky continues cloudy; the lake dull crimson. A patter of rain. It makes the fish crazy for a frolic and food. They shall have it—and so shall we! They nab the hooks: we snag three, four, by the ribs. They bite away as fast as I can throw out the line. Four, five, literally in as many minutes. A great cloud lowers over us. In the excitement a smart April shower, in June, surprises us, wets us pretty superficially and hurries us up and out, to escape. We wait many a weary hour to return to our sport; but no! Rain, rain! I have to get home two miles down lake and the northerly wind only stops the down patter at 10.30 P. M. These April-in-the-middle-of-June showers are not so innocuous to catarrhal throats, as I experienced for two days afterwards. But oh! that batch of seventeen or eighteen fine fish! that pays for all.

THE LITTLE SLEEPER OF AVOCA.

Monday, 18th.—Ah! Sweet God of infancy! This time brings a sad, suave recollection and anniversary—the sickness and death of little six-year-old

Beatrice Aungiers. How it tears the heart to recall
the mother's softer grief—grief dissolving in tears,
yet "would not be comforted, for her child is not!"
How contrasted with the father's sterner, tearless de-
spondency, ending in his clotting a ball of dirt and
throwing it on the lowering coffin with an undis-
tinguishable mutter, almost a curse, at the frenzied
moment of losing, so long, his first-born. They had
come from their pleasant yeoman's villa in rural
England, ivied, stonewalled. Their three children,
Beatrice, Laddie and baby Florence, were worried
by the sea sickness and the usual discomforts of a
voyage, a fourth round the globe; and too, by the
unpreparedness of prairie hotel life. All drooped.
Beatrice grew worse, commenced to wither—sweet
flower of beauty and innocence! wilted, dropped
her fair young head, like a dead rose on its stem,
and the sick spirit was gone!

I saw her but as the lily corpse, a little livid now,
lay in its white grave-clothes on the great bed over
the parlor. The sobbing mother led me in; we had
never seen one another before, but,

"A fellow-feeling makes all the world akin." ·

and hard would be the heart that throbbed not the
throb of sympathy with a blow such as this. We
stood beside it. But somehow, a child's remains
scarcely ever inspire me with grief, and tears dissolve into a bow of light above the sweet—aye,
sweet in death's cold arms, broken soul's tabernacle.

I smiled at the sleeper of Avoca, and thought of
the daughter of Jairus. In whiter robe we wound
her, in tiny cream coffin; and tho' something moved
to show of grief, we made her funeral and its touch-

ing circumstances like only the bearing of the little virgin **martyr**, sweet **smiling** in death, away from the amphitheatre of horror **to the calm** and holy catacombs. Only it had rained, and the poor grave was filled with mud **and** water; and oh! it hurt so to put that body in so foul a resting place. God heal smarting hearts! what a proof of the curse of sin even over the personally sinless, yet inheriting, fruit of sinful womb.

With deeper **sorrow** we laid her low; but then we had only sown a grain in God's Acre on the prairies, to be a ripe blessing on this colony and sanctify the soil for the future dead and the present **living**.

How I recall afterwards that the merciful God vouchsafed the life of baby Florence, sick unto death, thro' the intervention of our Lady of Lourdes; we consecrating the child to God and promising her full retirement from the world, with her discretionary **consent**. She lives now, a very darling, a little browned, **but** rosy-cheeked, sweet-eyed and chestnut-haired—fast filling the gone Beatrice's place and helping in her child's and artless way to nurse little Francis Eric, our God-son—sent some months later literally to refill the number at the fond mother's knee! Aye, Beatrice! well named, like the angels of God, sleep on with thy comrades of Avoca graveyard, little John and the two baby Catharines—lost babes.

> "Thy lovely companions
> Are faded and gone
> I'll not leave, thou lone one,
> To pine on the stem ;
> Since the lovely are sleeping,
> Go, sleep thou with them!"

18th—Evening.—There are sudden gusts of wind, some showers, **pretty** sharp **claps** of thunder, resembling our Middle States end of April or beginning of May. The birds do not seem to mind the weather. I hear them singing away.

Rt. Rev. Dr. Ireland visits us, principally to look after the Nuns of the Holy Child, who have come to take charge of an academy and parochial school at Avoca—much needed in these parts and destined to be the seminary of future branch houses throughout southern Minnesota, and maybe in neighboring States. God prosper them, and His cause is theirs!

Tuesday, 19*th.*—What a faultless day has this been! From the early sunrise, the first I have seen this season, until the late set, there has been scarcely the slightest fleck in the pale sunshiny sky; except **now, at** the last moments, a filmy veil of cloud has gathered **over** the western horizon **to** catch and embody the fine red light streaming over air and earth and sky.

Is it presumptuous to say this hyacinthine, spotless heaven, with its brilliant **sun in** the midst, like Gods' own Kohinoor, is the worthy bridal **ring of** the Maker's marriage with His unstained Virgin Earth! And the harmonies that have been playing in the air from the winds, **sweet** harpers, harping on all Nature's Æolian harps; mingling with the **sonorous hum of** gratitude **from man and** beast and **bird,** are all but the echo of the **sweeter symphonies Earth's Angels** have been harping **all the day** long!

And a worthy, calmly beautiful night has commenced **to** drop her curtain, ever so silently, in the south and east, thro' which shines in her moony **sheen the full orb.**

Here and there a few diminished stars pulse, feebly twinkling on the bosom of ether, but far removed from the Great White Throne of their earth-wedded queen. A greenish brightness still lingers on the upper edge of the light bank of vapors that shade off the path of the down-going of this day's sun. Blessed be God! "Holy in all His works, and wonderful in the heights!"

He has compensated for the simplicity of His Virgin Mother's prairie inheritance by the glories of the sky above it by day, and the quieter beauty of the nightly firmament.

Avoca, June 20th.—Two hunts, one fruitful of naught but exercise and giving a long ramble, musing along the great slough; another of an hour, dropping five birds and a mallard. They supplied our ecclesiastical supper for three priests and the Rt. Rev. Bishop.

Dr. Ireland opened the convent chapel to-day by celebrating the first Holy Mass in St. Rose's little original foundation on the prairies. The Mass was in honor of St. Angela Merici, foundress of the Ursulines, quite appropriate for the opening of a house of education. There being no other boarding school in all the wide distance from here to the Rocky Mountains, and only five or six little local Catholic schools, there is left a wide scope for the development of this community—of which more anon.

10.10 *P. M.*—All is still. Not a leaf stirs. Not a ripple, I think, on the lake. No sound but the soli-

tary "clack," "clack" from a disquiet water-bird,
the fiddle of the cricket, or the hiz-z-z of the mus-
quito! —

> "Te lucis ante terminum,
> Rerum Creator, poscimus
> Ut pro tua clementia '
> Sis Presul et Custodia." *

British Importations into Canadian North-west.

June 21, 22 *and* 23 were occupied by discussions
on the iniquity of the selfish British Government
sending paupers, criminals or others to Canada and
even to our shores. We must lump all in the following letter to the Boston Pilot, adding somewhat.

Avoca, Minn., June 24.

Editor of the Pilot:—Your, and the prominent
Catholic American press', late strictures on the importations of people from the British Isles to the
Canadian Northwest and even to our own States,
encourage me to advance some practical commen-
taries from the very neighborhood.

The seventy-odd delegates to the C. T. A. B.
Union of America, who were favored with free
tickets to Winnipeg and Manitoba last summer,
could give no good account of the trumpeted Red
River Valley or its contiguous territory in British

---

*) First verse of Hymn for Complins:
> "Thee, God, before the end of day,
> Creator of the worlds, we pray,
> Do for thine own sweet mercy sake
> Us under thy protection take."

America. They complained especially very bitterly of the swamped wheat fields, the alkalined water, and corroborated the detailed reports of correspondents to the Chicago Tribune and other practical sightseers.

Having made it **an object of** particular inquiry, on the testimony of several—two or three I specially remember—I have found that there are but patches of decently cultivatable land near the Red River, in fact at a distance **of** fifteen or twenty miles, the remainder **being** nothing more than

A GRAND NATURAL DRAIN

and swamp **of** the northern "divide." All the disadvantages **of** cold, wet, proximate untamableness, militate against this valley more and more strongly as you leave the middle line of even Minnesota and Dakota, **and above the British line;** and **as you as**cend through **Manitoba and Saskatchewan** into Athabaska-Mackenzie and the surroundings of Hudson's Bay, you are climbing the butt end of the North Pole.

In conversation to-day upon the English Government and syndicates' shipping of human cattle to Manitoba, Saskatchewan and Canadian Northwest, I propounded the question to a prominent dignitary, how it was possible **for** the imported poor to survive in those untamed wintry **wilds?** He agreed fully with me **that** it was hard to see how, taking into consideration, first, the awful degree of cold prevalent or, at least, incident there last season—up to 60 and 67 **degrees** below zero at periods, and a **late** cor-

respondent stating average winter cold at 40 degrees
below; secondly, the improvidence of the people
and want of shiftiness; thirdly, the companies' and
Government officials' cold business arrangements,
and lastly, the immense number shipped at once and
houseless.

To be sure, the same happens in great part in Dakota and Montana, when two lines of railroad (if
they do not lie in their reports), the Chicago and
Northwestern, and the C. M. and St. P. Railroads
have shipped, this spring, upwards of 200,000 to
Dakota.   There, no Government provision was
made; the demands far exceeded supplies both of
lumber for houses or sheds and provisions for man
and beast.   They explain the problem partially by
stating that the freight cars used for transport were
left the shiftless families for shelter.   But it would
be impossible.   We agreed that there was

Great Negligence,

and in fact, rascality on the part of the interested
Britishers in their anxiety to get rid of troublesome
"paupers."   Our own interested railroad officials and
land-grabbers on our side of the line, and the omnip-
otent syndicates on the British side, have studiously
avoided letting accounts of colonists' surely appall-
ing sufferings and present destitute condition creep
into the current press.   But facts from individuals
have leaked out and those living in Minnesota, who
have their ears open, know at least enough scattered
details about both the lands of the English Government and the appendant Red River Valley *to
warn off people who don't intend to commit suicide.*

If this whole *scheme—scheme*, indeed, of schemers of the abominable Irish-hating and poor-despising English officials—be not a practical repetition of the Cromwellian transportation to the colonies here and the Barbadoes, of the enslaved "Hell-or-Connaught"-bound prisoners of war, one would inquire the hair-splitting difference. If this be miscalled voluntary emigration, the fact that Ireland has come to her present pass by the fault of her seven-century oppressors gives the lie to the misnomer. Woe be to those so miserable, they have naught before them but a choice between British poor-houses and emigration to British America.

I might conclude by predicting very safely on the basis of some already accredited data of single families and small batches of colonists who, having gotten soon disgusted with much further North and West, actually fell back on the southern half of Minnesota, that there will be an ebb of emigration of this wild, wholesale, compulsory or foolishly voluntary emigration, as well as a flow. A great proportion of the best class and colonists of some means will inevitably have to use their common sense in ebbing back to this favored region—and the surrounding eligible prairies of Iowa and Nebraska, Southern Dakota and Montana. If some disadvantages of weather are trying, they are much less so in degree and by comparison even with our own public lands; while immeasurably, in fact incomparably, superior are matters of soil, weather, people, church facilities and schools of these parts as put in possible competition with the inhospitable regions of British rule.

At the last moment I have come across a map of public lands in the Dominion of Canada, printed at Montreal and by the authority of the Minister of the Interior, which lies as palpably under wilful mistakes about the summer and winter climate as any advertisement.

Just imagine, as here red and black lined, the same summer degree (sixty) from Victoria, U. S., around Great Slave Lake, past Deer and Winnipeg Lakes and down to forty-third parallel, a difference of about 20 degrees of latitude. And all the southern included region is marked in red letters, *Vast Region of Excellent Farming Lands.* Another enclosure, of course of more exquisite country, of 65 degrees Fahrenheit, from Peace River to off Long Island, N. Y. Happy New Yorkers! A winter of average 15 degrees (not said whether above or below zero) is divided off from Mt. Fairweather, Alaska, in southeastern course, to Rush City, Minn., and Ottowa, Can.; or of 20 degrees from top of Lake Michigan, past Toronto, to Albany, N. Y. And we write thus even with the admitted probability of the fact in sight, that the lines of cultivatable lands extend many more degrees north, in the region west of the great lakes and the Mississippi, than they do on either side of the Alleghanies in the East. . . .

To all this might be added, what the editor thought proper to omit, that Fr. Nugent of Liverpool and other ecclesiastics or prominent laymen, engaged in forwarding the interests of immigrants to the Canadian Northwest, do not, I believe, take the re-

sponsibility of answering for the wisdom or un-
charity of the speculators in human flesh and souls;
but use their influence and do personal work in
alleviation of the evils concomitant with any slighter
benefits accruing to the exported.

Importations into England are fraught with so
many proved dangers to the mercurial Celts, that a
very hard alternative is often chosen to avert actual
loss of souls—even, we may argue, by running risk
of loss of lives.

Besides (and I will freely admit the testimony of
all good men), who knows? There are those who
aver that life and a reasonable prosperity are among
the possibilities in settlements of such high latitudes.

After all, Horace Greeley and the New York
philanthropists, together with the majority of our
past geographists, had finally to admit that the race
rising in America is practically fitted for coping
with what would be chimeras with other peoples.
This has been demonstrated by the much more bearable and profitable habitability of the western plains
ascending to the Rockies than was credited or
credible to the uninitiated.

Therefore, the Pilot letter may be modified to the
extent to confess that, if interested "Englishers" and
their inhuman accomplices on both sides of the
water have at best only worldly and self-interested
motives in running the necks and souls of the un-
protected poor into jeopardy on the one side; on the
other, the candid opinions and believable experiences of our Prelates on both sides of the British
line here disagree to the point, that what some con-

demn, others as freely endorse and want to see carried out.

One probable argument, however, might be a subject for debate as for or against the proximate utility of lands and regions above described, viz: Why did not the stupendously powerful Hudson Bay Company, which had the actual dominion, like very monarchs, of all this British America, do something more, in their over two hundred years' possession, towards attempting the, to them, most profitable colonization of these wilds and steppes?

Maybe, it was not their interest or philanthropy, if you will, to let any of their power slip thro' their fingers by giving chances of free holdings? Possible.

But why, again, did they make such a tremendous row, in the long national contest concerning the fixing of our northern boundaries, about getting hold of the country included in Washington, Oregon Territory and present Montana, in fact, the whole line to the great lakes? if all the, now American, ground was not so much more valuable that they preferred it—and they knew the comparative values— to a great part of what they had indisputably possessed. Doubtful — but preponderating for the American side and views. We may safely conclude this prolix and vexatious discussion by adducing two of the highest authorities—one in spirituals, one in temporals—namely, Most Rev. Archbishop Lynch, in his second great letter, written at the suggestion of Pope Pius IX to the whole Irish Hierarchy; and Mr. John Sweetman. Here is the first: "We repeat again, that which could not be effected in Ireland by religious persecution, loss of lands and homes, social disabilities and starvation, has been accomplished here, in too many instances, by the enemy of all good and his agents. This forced emigration of an impoverished people into a new country whose inhabitants are overwhelmingly non-Catholic, has effected it." The second is the conclusion of "Recent Experiences:" "From the experience of this Company's efforts in Southwestern Minnesota, a country already largely settled and thoroughly intersected with railroads, I would conclude that any Government scheme to settle large numbers of destitute Irish families in the Canadian Northwest would be sure to fail. They would, no doubt, have the advantage of having free land, instead of having to pay twenty-five shillings the acre, but the price of land is a small portion of the expense of farming in the West, and they would have the disadvantage of being far from markets, and having a longer and colder winter."

Avoca, June 21st.—I said the second day's Mass in the Convent on St. Aloysius' feast—"the angelic youth, exemplar of innocence and chastity," given by Benedict XIII as "the patron special to studious youth." How fitly these two first Masses in honor of St. Angela, and the angels' compeer, will be rounded off in sweet trinity by the 30th of August's feast of our own St. Rose of Lima!—just the eve of school opening in September, when our colonists' bright children sing their own peculiar hymn to St. Rose, to invoke her blessing on school, home and heart!

ST. ROSE OF HOLY MARY.

When blush of light had shown
Thy face, like roses blown,
The Queen claimed thee Her own.
    St. Mary's Child!
Sweet in thy garden cell
Thine angel loved thee well,
And with thee came to dwell,
    Rose undefiled!

Till Jesus' garment hem
Did touch thy leafy stem,
Thou droopedst like to them
    Thorn-crucified;
Erecting sudden head,
With ardors blushing red,
When, "My heart's Rose"! He said.
    "Be thou my bride"!

Sweet God! whose dewy grace
Blessed dear Columbia's race
With meek St. Rose's face,
    And virgin bloom:
Make us, 'neath Convent guides,
Thine own devoted brides,
Scent all thy prairie wides
    With Christ's perfume!

June 22d.—Next day we had a hot but successful fish in the inlet, capturing some fourteen fat pickerel. Great flocks of jack snipes, a large game but rather tame bird, the size of a spring chicken, came sailing over the upper end of the lake, and we got two distant shots, failing to stop their progress.

MOONLIGHTING OVER THE PRAIRIE.

We rode in the face of the full orb of night. How beautiful to see the star of first magnitude rising fiery in the West, gradually increasing in splendor, advancing like the Star of Bethlehem, until the broad *headlight* bulged into the village with clanging of bell and scream of engine whistle, while the dull gold moon rose simultaneously in the East, chased with its defined chasms and moon mountains, great and broad ; anon lessening and silvering as it mounted, until its bright disk controlled all the sky! We heard a strange "click"-"click" over the drear prairie as we drove along. It precisely resembled a telegraph tapping, only in the quality of the sound, which was woody. It followed and came along near, and involuntarily a sort of superstitious creeping stole up our spines—the noise was certainly weird—doubled finally and seemed to be pursuing us. I wonder yet what it was, it could scarcely be a bird, certainly not a serpent, nor did it sound like any known insect.

We slept soundly after our drive. Night air is proved not unwholesome where there is no rank vegetation, nor foul standing water.

Finally, on the 23d, we went to Currie, the present representative of a county seat, late for Mass on St. John's day. I shot some birds at $8\frac{1}{2}$ P. M. and tried how late I could see to aim, spotting a plover at just 9 o'clock, but missing him. I could see the time by my small watch on the prairie to fully ten minutes or quarter past 9 o'clock.

June 24th.—Glorious St. John the Baptist! Pray for us. "*Solve polluti labii reatum, Sancte Joannes,*" indeed be our prayer for the purification of our guilty lips that talk so much and such foolishness! Says a Holy Father: "We hear naught of St. John

in Scripture, "save his conception and father's
oracle, his leaping in the womb and his voice in
the desert." . . . . "He had no childhood, but, above
nature, above his age, placed in his mother's womb,
he started life with the full measure of the age of
the fullness of Christ."

THREE WINTERS IN MURRAY COUNTY, MINN.

While at Currie, we learned some items of the
past three winters from a practical German trades-
man, wheelwright and carpenter. The first in 1880,
was the worst in memory; but even then commenced only late in February. For fifteen days,
people had no mails. Seventy men had to dig a
road by shoveling away the great banks of snow,
from Tracy, fifteen miles north, to get at a hundred
cords of firewood piled within three miles of Currie.
This winter you could not stir about much. In
'81–'82, the weather continued so mild that the
$10,000 Currie Church, all frame, was commenced
after Christmas and put under roof by the following
March. Men worked for weeks together without
fire in their shops. There was notably not enough
snow for sleighing the whole season thro', tho' the
roads continued frozen.

In '82–'83, in spite of the six or seven short severe
blizzards, there was fine driving, of course in sleighs
or slides, most of the time. The great snow storms
lasted but one, or at most, two days, tho' I have it
from a sufferer, that he had been blocked on a train
for three days and had to live on pretty hard tack
till relieved. It is not coldest during the blizzards,

the thermometer seldom ranging to 18 or 28 degrees below zero. The coldest here recorded last winter was 35 degrees below, ten or fifteen degrees lower than the worst at this writing, January, 1884, and the actual point reached, even in the Ohio valley this winter. By contrast, we had at Avoca on Wednesday last 114 degrees in the sun; on Friday 86 degrees in the shade. First bouquet of prairie roses!

It is a singularity that many a time, as is the case commonly in the Ohio valley, there is decided winter weather in the shape of profuse snow falls or bitter, biting spells, only after Christmas, or even sometimes not before Candlemas, on the 2d of February. So here, there are severe frosts and freezing, but these are not so violent but, winter about, public work, building, even plastering with stoves to dry gradually by, may not be continued far past the fall season proper. In fact, in St. Paul, Minneapolis, and other large cities, housebuilding goes on every winter almost without interruption, except for severer intervals.

This may happen out on the prairies too, as I have learned from honest mechanics.

In looking over a record, which a prominent farmer and grazer, Mr. Dan. Murphy, of Avoca, kept day by day for the past two winters, springs and falls, I was astounded to find a large proportion of days marked as "fair," "fine," "very fine," and so soft as "pleasant" in the heart of the hardest season, viz: about January and February of the worst winter. Very bad weather is the exception here as elsewhere in the habitable agricultural districts, according to eye and touch witnesses ; nor does it last so long, ordinarily, as strangers imagine or believe.

It would, however, be folly to deny that it is very cold almost all the winters. Long cultivated districts, especially tree-planted, do seem to change temperature for the better.

It is equally true that there is no such thing as what is vulgarly termed a "let-up" to the dry persistent grip of winter proper. There are indubitably dreadful snow storms betimes, lasting for several days—in effect by exception for a week—in which it is dangerous, not only for foot passengers and riders or drivers to be out far from help, but even for the great iron horse.

Adrian, Nobles Co., Minn., June 25th to 27th.—Rev. Wm. Keul, pastor of Avoca, and I have just returned from an overland trip to Adrian, Nobles County, a progressive colony town. We are tired out for the nonce. Badger Lake, on the way to Iona, Murray County, with cross-armed tree, always consulted as a guide across the southwestern prairie, is quite full of water. Slough would be its more proper name, for it is very sedgy yet. Not many ducks on it, tho' in full season. The goodly number of trees that fringe the western shores would, if trimmed and cared for, mark the place with a parklet of uncommon beauty. It commands a fine prospect over the lake and surrounding roll of hills.

Fr. McDonnell's Home of the Sacred Heart.

Father McDonnell, the projector of the Home of the Sacred Heart for orphans at Iona, has a new matron over his embryo establishment, assisted by several maids to attend the inmates, now consisting

of some five little fellows of tender age. The Rev.
Superior is also factotum in temporal matters of the
neighborhood, being, I believe, a civil magistrate,
and certainly the local postmaster and storekeeper.
In this latter capacity he is famed the country over
for selling very low and cheap for cash—perhaps
sometimes on "tick," the good Father!

The nine thousand acres turned over to him at the
division of the Avoca colony land comprise some
fairly rolling sections, notably about the seven-or-
eight-house village of Iona, around the promontory-
like front of which flows a small stream. There
was once practical question about settling some of
the Avoca township farmers and other new comers
in and about the supposedly government land near
here. A few took steps to secure it, and maybe one
or two actually lived on it a time. The tract was
however in dispute between the railroad companies;
and it was perhaps fortunate enough that the specu-
lating parties did not invest, as it has come to ear
that the C. St. P. M. and O. Railroad Company, in
final suit, has had the land adjudged to them as part
of their bonus.

Quite a picturesque railroad trestle fronts the
Home, a large square frame, built originally for a
hotel, with spacious rooms for store, office, refectory
and kitchen down stairs; and the upper story divided off into small and larger apartments for sleeping, storage, etc.

We had occasion to find out that the innocent
looking stream circling about the town limits is
nearly up to a horse's neck, viz: by our vehicle
being nearly foundered in the deep narrow sink.
The water is clear and sweet.

On the borders of the great sections of the farm lies a beautiful, quadrangular lake, "Cora Belle," if you please, wherever it tripped up on such an æsthetic name. In very deed a fine expanse of water, level shores, deep, and half a mile square. To the right approaching it from the village is a smaller lakelet with little round tufted islands, quite taking in their light green softness and grace. Both are the great haunt of grand flocks of wild geese, of course, thousands of duck, and particularly frequented by a singular large white crane, of good edible quality. We knew the sandhill crane, which is properly a land-lubber, is prized as a delicacy; not so of water cranes.

Going to and from Adrian, we made a thirty-mile-sided parabola; thus seeing upwards of fifty, near sixty miles of the borders of Murray County and a gross half of Nobles County. The land seems ordinary prairie, rather inclined to sudden elevations and depressions, flat levels of miles of watery bottoms stretching frequently between the lines of knobby rolls, which latter are mostly thin soiled and gravelly. Deep sloughs and water cuts diversify the landscape and spoil many sections.

ADRIAN (MINNESOTA) COLONY.

Mr. Wm. J. Onahan, Secretary of "The Irish Catholic Colonization Association," in his third annual report, May, 1882, furnishes the preliminary information of this Catholic settlement: "Rev. C. J. Knauff, pastor of the Adrian (Minn) Colony, gave an account of his charge. The colony was established in 1877 by Bishop Ireland, of St. Paul, who obtained the right from the St. Paul & Sioux City Railroad Company to sell 70,000 acres of land in Nobles County, on the Worthington and Sioux Falls branch. In that year there were but two houses in Adrian, and now there are four hundred. Father Knauff was the first Catholic and the first priest to settle in the place, and now there are two hundred and fifty Catholic families there. It is situated on a high plateau forming the divide between the Mississippi and Missouri rivers, and the soil is very rich. The products are wheat, corn, flax, barley and oats. The heavy rains of last season reduced the crops, but the prospects for a big yield this year are very good. Two-thirds of the population are Irish, and one-third of German nationality."

Accustomed to levels on the prairie, you look down astonished at the cattle and sheep grazing in the low bottoms near Adrian. We met on the journey the largest herd of cattle I have ever seen on the open prairie, as many as two hundred head of beeves and some three hundred sheep, herded by a cowboy on horseback and a shepherd dog. A large field of waving rye sways ready for the sickle, and rising as high as four and one-half to five feet. Barley is nearly as far advanced. Wheat seems some fourteen to eighteen inches. Vegetables are getting plentiful in well-weeded gardens.

Adrian has so many as six hundred inhabitants, rises tierwise on a gentle slope—good school building, worth $2,000, and Catholic establishment and comfortable priest's residence, surrounded by nurseries of trees, a modicum giving tolerable shade.

The pastor, Rev. C. J. Knauff, claims (as previ-

ously reported) two hundred and fifty families here
and in surrounding missions, five in number. This
learned gentleman is also a member of the great
Colonization Board of Chicago, in charge of numerous prairie colonies. We were much jaded by the
tedious ride with a backless buggy over the uneven,
almost roadless district. We kept the prairie most
of the way, passed some sloughs up to the hub in
black loam; and finally thro' sheer fatigue and back
ache I sat in the front booth of the buggy, leaning
my back against the dash board with my legs
thrown over the seat. Returning, we had a "lazy"
back arranged after long manufacture; gave our
poor horse a new rig and net, and enjoyed cooler
weather. One finds it can become uncomfortably
warm riding hours out, even while it remains cool
and pleasant indoors. We killed and messed on
eleven curlews and as many plovers on the way.
The number of shots fired (we counted for curiosity)
was about thirty-five; so some two-thirds hit, on the
wing.

Avoca, June 28th.—Back to our Avoca; I have
scarcely begun the day; woke at 5; arose at 5¾; Holy
Mass at 6½; served another at 7. Fr. Koeberl, the
first colony pastor, is visiting us—a fine, tall, well-
formed Austrian, with the characteristic blonde hair,
fresh as new silk, and bluish eyes. He had a rough
mission here—a pair of small box rooms to lodge in
and board at the hotel, such as it was.

How the glorious sunny days follow one another,
each finer than the succeeding; some so magnificent with glittering, sparkling shine, coolish, vivifying breeze, haloing influence on the shrubbery on

the lake banks: the simple stalks of green waving
here and there, rendered vocal by the multifarious
calls and catches of birds of sea and land, that one
is tempted to shout aloud for very joy and exultation: "This is the day that the Lord hath made; let
us exult and rejoice therein. My soul doth mag-
nify the Lord. And all that is within me bless
His Holy Name." Thus one lives at times intensely
I can scarce contain myself, and after such exterior
joy I am set musing, oh! so sweetly!

29th.—Sts. Peter and Paul! How cold we are in
presence of such ardor of words and deeds! What
right ambition have I that with St. Chrysostom, I
do not weep over the words of the ardent apostles,
impetuous, human Peter, diviner Paul—but both
after their conversion. Give me but a throb of their
devotion to the cause of Jesus the Christ, living in
them, working by them. Have mercy, clement
Lord, on all thy consecrated servants this day and
forever!

AUSTRIAN COLONISTS.

We came home late last evening from the really
beautiful family of Austrians, the Steiners, living towards the Des Moines country, five miles east. We
had some fracas tho' on the way with an indignant
Norwegian who wanted to collar us for riding thro'
his grain field. Fact is, we had got mixed up in
finding a proper road and seeing worn tracks thro'
the wheat drove ahead regardless of naught but our
direction. But the fellow was a sorehead and
wanted to pick a quarrel. Expostulating with him
mildly we could not allay his anger and he threat-

ened us with prosecution for trespass. We let him
lather away and bade him—go to the judge. He
was very curious to see what one of us had just shot
on his premises, as the chicken season was not open
and he was itching for a chance to indict us for
law-breakage. But we had the inside track ; they
were only plovers.

But our Austrians! How singular, or rather how
natural, to find such genuine worth and attractive
moral beauty in one of these low box houses of a
single room and kitchen—with naught to recom-
mend the inmates but their Christian manners and
trifles of attention.

Here is apparently a rough man of the prairie,
who, with his unshaven face, bristly mustache and
red complexion, has withal the actual politeness of
reverence and true humility, mingled with, and
grounded on, an unobtrusive charity. There is no
genuine politeness and all is hollow, without these
three virtues. Waiting on the table and changing
the common stone china plates, his kindly eye of
bluish grey, and intelligent person become an object
of complaisance, tho' he says only: "Bitte (please
take this or that") as he relieves you of something
and hands another, adding as he heaps your plate:
"Essen Sie, nur, Herr Pfarrer, was Ihnen gefællt,
und lassen Sie dass andere!" (Eat only what you
like, sir, and leave the rest.")

And his practical wife, a true woman, who is a
good cook of her specialty of Austrian dishes, and
careful housekeeper, priding simply in her art without least offense, aye, only for your gratification.
She is, we find, an educated woman, cultivated, un-

derstanding person, who knows her business in hand and is only artlessly curious to know of things pertinent to utility.

Her care of her three hearty children, beautiful in their prairie rosiness and plump health, is only of a moral piece with her deferential conduct towards her husband, and her heartfelt passionateness in kissing on her knees the hands of each of the priests, asking their blessing for a purpose. With homeliness tho' some regularity of features, in her simple dark calico, and without an ornament, fresh from over the stove, cooking our meal, she is attractive. Her smile is sweet when she shows her regular teeth and her eye kindles with pleasure and pride over the honor done her by her loved "Herren Pfarrer." In the beauty of her prairie home, and its to her all-in-all inmates, the woman's untainted womanliness makes her lovely and lovable.

Dear Christian hearts, willing hands, healthy bodies and sound minds! Here they dwell on the rolling banks of the meandering Des Moines river; in view of their flourishing crops and small herd of lowing cattle, which they are but keeping however, their souls clinging to God and truth first ; succeeding moderately in this world's goods, they are an example and a sample of the all but inimitable good German Catholic colonists.

I was repaid for my necessitated promenade between twelve and one last night. The sweet day had lingered so long, long over the favored summer plains. Little strings of coral, amber, amethyst and

pearl dotted and fringed the horizon. The rolling
smoke grew pink in the setting rays. The sun disappeared and the shades crept majestically over a
section of the east, then over a larger and ever larger
half-circle. But on to even 10 o'clock, the last faint
rays played on the western limits of the billowy
fields. I went to bed, but could not rest   12, midnight. How only mildly, warmly bright, the glories
of the heavens, the branching milky way, feathery
silver ; Lyra, in middest heaven, enthroned ; Sirius
sharply brilliant; the Dipper broadly luminous.
How near seemed the soft pulse of the starry host
on the bosom of ether! Could not an attentive ear
hear the symphony of these God-worthy spheres?
An awe of divine presence crept over me, and a
thrill shook the sanctuary of my soul.

How prayerful the night. Alone with God and
his silent, majestic creation. I heard the solitary
scale of the bittern in the slough. A prairie lark
gave vent to a single, trumpet-like call. A dog
bayed the rising moon with a single bark. I stood
alone awake of all the inhabitants of these limitless
regions. And these were but imitative cries of the
soul towards its Creator! I bowed struck with over-
powering emotion, bent the knee and recited the
8th Ps.: "Domine, Dominus, Noster." Holy Trinity, save me ! "Thy magnificence is elevated above
the heavens. I will behold thy heavens, the works
of (but) thy fingers: the moon and stars which thou
hast set." And I am of those "whom thou hast
made little less than the angels, crowned with glory
and honor and set over all the works of thy hands!"
Tho' this last applies only to the perfect man—

Christ Jesus—until we shall have grown to his stat-
ure, "been placed over many things" when "found
faithful over few."

WHITE HEAT AND CRUEL HUNT.

30th June—1st July.—Some grass is ready to cut
in the first dry sloughs. A few are cutting in
patches. The degree of heat, growing greater each
day for half the week, is wonderful for the prairie.
Were it not for the almost continuous breeze it
would be insufferable without shade. 97 degrees in
the middle half of the day. From 95 to 98 degrees
throughout Southwestern Minnesota, reaching, I
hear, a hundred, in some localities, the hottest for
the day of any part of the United States. I suffered
from it hunting yesterday evening; could make out
but a meagre tea. We killed some nineteen birds
in this and the morning's passing hunt.

The chicken-like plover, how confidently they
strut in my neighborhood this sunny, Sunday morn,
regardless, ignorant of my bloodthirsty persecution
of the feathered kind. I could all but side with
Thomson in his Seasons where he writes :

"This falsely-cheerful barbarous game of death,
This rage of pleasure, which the restless youth
Awakes, impatient with the gleaming morn: . . .
Man . . . with the thoughtless innocence of power
Inflamed, beyond the most infuriate wrath
Of the worst monster that e'er roamed the waste,
For *sport alone* pursues the cruel chase,
Amid the beaming of the gentle days.
Upbraid, ye ravening tribes, our wanton rage,
For hunger kindles you, and lawless want;
But lavish fed, in Nature's bounty rolled,
To joy at anguish and delight in blood
Is what your horrid bosoms never knew."

Very appropriate if proper exceptions be allowed.
It seems indeed a cruel alternative. The saints of
old and of our own times have been noted for their
kind treatment of, and familiarity with, beasts and
birds and fish. It is like the two things to choose
between in answering blow by blow even in self-
defense, or in allowing the smiter to strike the other
cheek. The latter is more perfect, but the former
allowed. I would not deprive these innocents of
life for mere sport's sake, and will not wantonly de-
stroy them, fearful of the threat of the Holy Writ :
"The life of the beast shall be required at thy
hands." Shall not even they stand in judgment
against us, tho' St. Thomas teaches none shall be
resuscitated!

I found a sort of "cockscomb" growing on tall
underbrush by the higher lake banks. And more
worthy of note, what but a genuine wild "Sweet
William" with its pleasant, red, five-petaled blos-
somlets and bursted, sheath-like, striped oatheads!
The dwarf wild roses dot the prairie and lake
shores in all stages from tiny buds to full-blown
pink and white five-leaves. The very grasses are
wondrous, finer far than Hungarian or ordinary
material for aluming for winter bouquets. Some
tossing feathery plumes of exquisite gloss and fine-
ness grow in patches—filmy textures like tangled
spiderwebs hide the dark soil of slough beds; dozens
of varieties of heads and stems, partitions and branch-
ings make the prairie bloom without blossom

Two more Nuns of the Holy Child arrived by
last night's train, bringing also a young Cuban to

summer with them for her health and to avoid the
plague that is prevalent in her island-home of the
West Indies. The number of nuns is now seven;
but Mother Waldburga, the Mother Vicaress of the
whole Society, after settling the property of the
Community, will leave its organization and the
school to gentle Mother St. Antony. There is remarkable refinement combined with veriest industry
in these ladies of this Anglo-American Congregation. Their notable Anglicisms are pretty, and they
seem withal to have the push of Americans.

Comic Characters.

We have them on the prairie as elsewhere and
maybe, as Addison argues, our laughter at them
proceeds from our pride that we are smarter than
they. Here is an original but not imaginary hero of
the cap and bells. He was imported from—you may
guess where. Very broad-faced, deep-whiskered,
narrow between the eyes, with tongue hung like a
clapper, our extravagant braggart, poor fellow, is, if
not happy in his ignorance, very deep set in his
opinions—if always a responsible agent. Book-
learned in part and with a smattering of experience
in odds and ends, specially however a sort of expert
in hunting and a fair "shot," he sets his mouth going
as by machinery on his pet subjects, and gets out
the absurdest oddities in neatly trimmed phrase.

"Ho! do ye know? my dog, pure Irish setter, is
perfect. Never knew him to fail to set a bird in
due range. You must guard against saying the
least word to him on the field." Well, that dog has
the queerest look and manner one ever saw in a ca-
nine. He is sharp, brisk, but his eye wanders and

his head seems fuddled, if his brain is not addled.
For, by my fowling piece! if I didn't take him out
one day and he managed with great halloing to "put
up" two chickens tolerably. The next thing, left to
himself, he ran over six birds, all hand-running but
one, and this one he ran into in plain sight of all but
himself, after having set him for nearly a full minute
just preceding.

"Oh! I thought he was perfect. He never does
the like with me." I doubted this considerably.
But what was added proved the dog smart: "Do ye
know"—with a sly wink—"that dog knows a gentleman at sight, and won't pay the least attention to a
soldier or a policeman!"

But halt, lest we commit the fault we condemn.
Still it's all in good humor and only observations on
particular studies in human nature. What if we in-
terlard such with real nature notes, mindful ever of
St. Augustin's dinner-table motto: "Whoso back-
bites his neighbor is not welcome at this board."
"Quisquis proximum carpit absit a mensa"—or such
words.

About this time was published the following letter, with these head and sub-captions, by the veteran
editor of the New York Freeman's Journal:

MINNESOTA:

ITS CLIMATE: BUT ESPECIALLY, A GRAND EDUCA-
TIONAL ESTABLISHMENT.

Editor N. Y. Freeman's Journal: Dear Sir—
Whilst some of your contemporaries are flooding

their columns with "Catholic colony prospects in
Florida," some jottings from the opposite **point** of
the horizon will not seem intrusive. The agricultural and educational items (published in the Philadelphia "Catholic Standard") which I sent from Avoca
last fall were meagre, and I shall not be longer now—
not much. Last winter here, from all **accounts,** was
most **blizzardly affected—the very extreme** pole of
the winter **preceding.** There is no denying that an
earnest **business** blizzard is a fearful demon—not so
fearful, **however, as your** demoniacal tornadoes south
and east **from here. But what's a blizzard to me**
any more than a State penitentiary? I do not **expect**
to get into either **one, if I know** myself, **and it's**
pleasant looking at a grand, blowing snowstorm
from a cosy room. Have a right and tight house,
not too **fashionable, but very sensible; watch the**
signs **of the clerk** of the weather out of the corners
of both eyes, **and** drive like **fury, if out, in a** certain
direction **of** a house, and you **need** fear nothing
much more serious than chilblained toes and numb
fists. **Only** look out for your nose, if peculiarly
Roman! **Only** one man in this region froze to death,
and he was **brimful** of whisky. And if there be
any one thing a person ought to avoid when traveling in fierce winter weather—here as elsewhere—
that thing is throwing a spirit flask to your head
every few miles — especially **when you feel be-**
numbed. Walk and drink **water** is nature's pre-
scription—or take a few swallows of good butter **or**
some good sweet oil.

The spring, indeed, seems backward; **not excep-**
tionally so, **however, as travelers up through Indi-**

ana or Illinois, with their prairies floating in water
and many wheat fields ploughed up for corn, evidence. When those conjuncting planets stop fool-
ing with our atmosphere, North and South, we may
expect more normal seasons. As to the prevalence
of spring rains out this far, I believe, from close observation, that, unpleasant as they are, they are
necessary for this sand-mixed and high-rolling soil
thoroughly to modify it for the short, hot summer,
coming on like a thief in the night.

In any case, crops, except corn, are not looking
so bad, though low yet; on the contrary, you will
hear good farmers, who have put their time in and
have a fairly rolling section, report other grains as
prospering. We have some lettuce, greens, onions
and even a few strawberries in gardens.

REMINISCENCES OF KENTUCKY.

Passing along the undulating farms, partly wooded,
partly prairie, from Winona, on the Mississippi, to
Heron Lake, almost on a direct west line, I found
things looking charming indeed—the vegetation
only about six weeks behind the blooming fields and
wooded heights of my native Kentucky, thro' which
I had just finished a five weeks' trip from Cincin-
nati to Paducah by water, and inland from the
mouth of the Tennessee to the glorious regions of
the Blue Grass. I could not fail to notice the precise resemblance of the best Minnesota prairie with
our finest farm and grazing lands along the "Beautiful River"—but especially about our Lexington and
the valley of the Kentucky river, minus, of course,
the park-like, magnificent forest trees, the dusty

pikes, white fences in the green meadows, and the
lordly country villas.   It is worthy of incidental remark that the seventeen counties of middle Kentucky, bordering on the one side the Blue Grass
region and the Big Bone district, and in between
the great coal belt about Green River and the Cum-
berland, were, in the first settlement of the State,
found to be pure prairie, devoid of all but coarse
grass, and roamed over by buffaloes, frequented by
deers and the haunt of large game birds.

Outside of this, there are sections interspersed between neighboring hills on which old inhabitants
say you could not find a riding-switch forty years
ago.   As all this is now grown up in dense forests,
and finely timbered, may not a like event happen —
mutatis mutandis — in the *breaks* of the Northwest?
Thus the timber question may solve itself after the
first plantings of trees shall have grown a decade old
and form nature's seminary for propagation.   The
timbered portion of Minnesota, containing nearly all
the best forest trees, is itself not too far away to
supply the winged seeds to the breezes from the East
and South carrying them West and North.   The comparative stoppage of the formerly most destructive
prairie fires will then also allow the tree-seeds to pul-
ulate in the open soil; and the frequent rains largely
supplement the efforts of man and nature to reclothe
the wide areas with the fruits of arboriculture.
Further, it's remarkable that the largest oaks, maples,
hickories and ash trees of the older Kentucky forests
will not, ordinarily be found to be more than from
fifty to one hundred years of age; so that old farmers
tell us they believe a much larger area was, say a
hundred years back, pure prairie.

Eight or ten new arrivals this spring, and in Fulda about a dozen new houses built. This much about materialities.

SCHOOLS FOR CATHOLIC CHILDREN

are a notable deficiency in these regions outside of the largest cities and greater towns. In the small towns, out in the farming sections, and even in the colonies there are not and have not been hitherto any provisions for Catholic education. The ubiquitous public system of colorless instruction has grappled the soil and followed the onward march of the invading railroads. One coming from the southern Dioceses, either west or east, or even the German-settled archiepiscopal territory adjoining Canada, feels the absence keenly, and his first regret is that Catholics had not prepossessed the educational facilities, and led instead of dragging behind in the first school enterprises.

When the majority of town and country districts are schoolless for Catholics, even if the greater number are of the faith, it will hardly do to solve the education problem by grafting a sickly catechetical instruction on the tail-end of the school-day. Doses of Christian doctrine have been tried on both Sundays and week-days, and been found wofully wanting in supplying backbone to our air-poisoned children. Certainly reasons there are for the slower multiplication of our schools this far out — one chiefly lying in the incredibly rapid increase of population of both State and Church, and in the newness of Church establishments, especially in the colonies.

When we state that the population of Minnesota
has increased over a *thousand* per cent. in ten or
twelve years, and the Church has spread her tent
and widened her borders in proportion—the priests
amounting in St. Paul Diocese to 140, churches 189,
schools 79, with 9,418 scholars—one may understand
the growth of twenty-five years' **Catholic life.**

A GREAT BOON.

And now, to come to some particulars about one
of the oldest of the existing colonies. The wedge
has been entered on this, the fifth anniversary of
the foundation of Avoca, by the introduction of the
Order of the Nuns of the Holy Child Jesus, of whom
a colony of six or seven have lately arrived under
Mothers Walburga and St. Antony, to start a boarding and day school. The building used hitherto as
a hotel, and a really handsome and roomy two-and-
one-half story frame, is being proximately arranged
for the reception of scholars. With such re-arrange-
ment and the portioning off of a large plat of ground
near the Lake of St. Rose of Lima, the Lincoln
Hotel will scarcely know itself in the beautiful Convent of Avoca. Foresight and foreknowledge have
been brought to bear on the scheme by the matter
having been thoroughly examined and agreement
made with Right **Rev.** Dr. Ireland by the Rev.
Mothers last fall; so that, relying on Providence
and being backed up by this already pretty large
community of Catholics, slowly but surely increasing, and the whole territory of Southwestern Minnesota to draw upon for boarders, there is certainly
reasonable prospect of success, when at least the

colonies shall have been educated up to a proper
patronage of the God-sent institution. Some fifty
children have attended the district school at Avoca.

If no brilliant success be its portion in the first
few years, provided only a decent maintenance be
secured, it will not be unlike the remainder of God's
foundations on this earth, grounded on faith and
patience, and seconded by an industry, practicalness,
and thoroughgoingness characteristic of these experienced religious.

A PRACTICAL PRIEST'S SUGGESTION.

Whatever drawbacks there are otherwise—and
some there do exist, humanly speaking—may, we
think and hope, be counteracted by a *lift* from the
East. How? you will ask. Well, to say simply the
truth, admitted by candid people who have tested it,
this being the highest elevated plateau in the plain
running parallel with the Mississippi River and
stretching on to the Arctic Ocean—securely proven
by its being the water-divide between the gulf and
the ocean—it is one of *the healthiest places on this
continent. One of them*—I don't say the only one.
Sensible men, outside of land speculators, colonizers,
or even physicians, from all but every clime, have
had delighted experience of it, and your Southern
resorts are slowly—and not so slowly either—being
abandoned for the purer, drier, less malarial, better
oxygenized and curative plains of the Northwest. I
have nothing, the least, to do with colonization, land
sales, railroads, or speculation, and I can freely say
on the word of a man and a priest that, judging from
my own experience for this, now the second sum-

mer, and that of persons scattered all over Southern Minnesota, I have nowhere found the relief from chronic dyspepsia, nor others from incipient consumption, to be had here for the asking, and the running a little over these dustless and smokeless prairies. And on this subject I would refer the incredulous reader to the most timely articles of Dr. Felix L. Oswald on the "Remedies of Nature—Consumption," in the May and June numbers of the Popular Science Monthly—*et alibi*. "God's medicine"—the certainly best of all—is here in abundance: the three requisites of *moderate diet* (until you climb to a Minnesota appetite!), plenty of pure water and the royalest exercise.

The innumerable lakes teem with varieties of some of the sweetest fish that ever swam; the prairies are alive with game nearly the year round—certainly for three seasons—and fish can be speared by the hundred pounds in winter; and what roads we do have, barring a few sloughs now and then in early summer or spring!

So, my plea is for encouragement, practical and pressing advice to be given to our thousands of delicate girls and women, to invade the West in quest of health, as men do for gold. Health is the better of the two, and more needed. Here is a spot for persons able to travel (and it's no trick to get out here from Chicago in twenty-four hours), and wanting to join practical education with a supply of physical and mental health that will be stock enough for half a score of years. On particular inquiry, I can say with confidence, that there is nothing in the regulations of the Holy Child Nuns which would prevent them from receiving members of other sisterhoods,

who might be sent for their health to these parts,
if their stay be but limited to a season at a time.
Many lives of our delicate Southern religious might
be saved or prolonged by a summer here.

In the name of common sense, nay, in the holier
name of the God of Nature! send your drooping
daughters here to the Convent of Avoca, and as sure
as pure air, glow of exercise, attractions of unpolluted Nature, can dispense with doctors and their
doings, their cheeks will acquire the noted Minnesota rose that blooms only this side the Mississippi;
their delicate bodies will brace up, and they will
bound like the roe. There will simply be no controlling their vigorous appetites, when they shall
have been properly acclimated, and—well, that's
what they will come for, besides their education,
which will not fail under the hands of these religious
ladies, who evidently do not believe in fringes and
folderollery, but educate for life." . . . . .

NUNS OF THE HOLY CHILD JESUS.

A circular of the Nuns of the Holy Child Jesus'
School accompanied this letter, in which intimation
was made that a midwinter vacation, instead of the
one in midsummer, would be introduced as a new
feature suitable to changed circumstances.

DOMESTIC TEACHING.

And it was dared to be announced that these religious ladies would teach on the practical basis of including woman's general work among their scholars,
and insist with the Rt. Rev. Bishop's express agreement, the girl pupils should be practiced in sewing;

cooking, ironing, etc. It is a new departure in this country and a needed innovation or rather return to common sense principles in education. I will not weary by introducing Sr. **Mary Frances Clare, the famous Nun** of Kenmare's, **practice** in her poor **schools in** Ireland, **as** told by the Philadelphia Press correspondent:

"You see, sir," she said, "whilst **there** is a great deal of talk about doing **good** for the Irish peasant, **there** is very little real **work** being done. Now the women are exceedingly **ignorant.** Certainly **it is** not their own **fault, poor** things, **but that is all the more reason for teaching** them. **There are very** few **girls or women in** this very surrounding **country** who **can make their** husband **or brother a good shirt.**

No Fresh Eggs in Ireland.

"An egg is fresh sometimes, yet one seldom **gets a fresh egg in** Ireland. **People attribute this to the climate. That is not the** cause. **The women don't know how to preserve** them at all; so, too, with butter. **Well then, my idea is** to teach all practical house-keeping **knowledge, to train** house-servants, to educate girls in the art of cooking, **and to prepare** them for good, useful, intelligent wives and servants, so that when they go out to America you **good peo-** ⁄ **ple** will find **them** serviceable.

"**In this way we hope to return,** in a very small way, the **charity your** people are giving toward **the school.** Whatever I find a girl most fit for I intend **to train her for.** The school will not **be a patent** groove machine. The education, the book-learning, **will be** confined to practical **English** branches only.

"To sustain this school the girls must work. I

therefore propose to buy knitting machines and
make knit goods for the market. These goods are
not to be sold as charity goods. I shall compete in
open market, and no other way. If the work won't
pay that way it will be a failure. Sisters or nuns
will be taught by professionals, and they will instruct
the girls. So many hours a day will be devoted to
such work as will bring in a remuneration for the
support of the school. Of course, there will be regular hours for books, but they will not be many.

"I am seeking to do a practical good, and not
to found a great school of learning. Besides the pupils we shall have as boarders, we will utilize all the
women about the neighborhood who can spend their
now idle time in learning practically needed home
accomplishments."

Here are some religious from Switzerland, who
are braver yet : "The Theodosian Sisters of the
Convent of Holy Cross, Canton of Zug, Switzerland, have hit upon a programme of female education
which ought not to pass unnoticed. Instead of
training their pupils into lady barristers and lady
doctors, they aim at turning out practical mothers
of families and thrifty house wives. Thus, cooking
in all its departments; the art of carving and serv-
ing up; the uses of the various market supplies; the
elements of household chemistry; the scientific ar-
rangement of kitchen, stores, cellars, and pantries;
the profitable laying out of vegetable gardens; the
methods useful in the laundry; the cure of infant
diseases; the rearing of babies—are the chapters
which they courageously write at the head of their
programme of studies. And this is no mere boast,
for their teaching was tested by lady visitors, and

pronounced most satisfactory. The confidence of parents rewards the efforts of the good Sisters; they closed the year 1881 with ninety-five boarders, and the year 1882 with one hundred and thirteen."

July 2*d.*— And our Lady's beautiful visitation. Our Convent children join with the little ones of the whole colony in singing a home-made hymn to their patroness, St. Rose of Lima, as fanciedly connected with our Blessed Mother's visit to her prairie children :

AMERICA'S ROSE.

This visitation day
We cull each flowering spray
On prairie, lake and way
  Of sweet St. Rose:
Pink buds and white to bloom,
Fit types of virgin womb.—
St. Rose's breath perfume
  The flower she chose!

Who hath but virgin been
Exults a Mother Queen;
John Lily's Bud hath seen
  On Jesse's rod;
Elizabeth does know
What prophets dimly show,
And greets her, bending low,
  Who bears her God.

To seraph's lyric strain
St. Rose hies o'er her plain
To join Queen Mary's train
  Ere she departs:
Her feet a carpet tread
Of green with blossom spread,—
St. Rose shall crown her head
  With children's hearts.

How much more applicable to the religious teacher than to even good Mrs. Hemans, the poetess, are these lines addressed to the latter by Mrs. Sigourney:

> "Every unborn age
> Shall seek thee with its household charities;
> The hoary sire shall bend his deafened ear
> And greet thy sweet words with his benizon;
> The mother shrines thee as a vestal flame
> At the lone temple of her sanctity,
> And the young child who takes thee by the hand
> Shall travel with a surer step to heaven."

Avoca, July 2.—The heat was so sensible all day yesterday that the priest giving benediction of the most Blessed Sacrament thought proper to warn the congregation to pray God to avert any calamity that might be impending, as he feared some dreadful storm was brewing. At the vespers the singers fairly gave out from exhaustion, and the services had to be shortened.

The thermometer stood at 96 degrees in the shade from 10 A. M. (110 degrees in the sun, increased at its height to 120 degrees), and culminated at 97 degrees in the Nun's piazza at 4¼ or 4½ P. M. It subsided to 85 degrees by 9 P. M. I was much fearful of a storm, if not of a regular cyclone. The sun shed a yellowish shine in the afternoon; the horizon at all points but towards the West seemed closing in upon us, and the wind was warmish until near six o'clock, when, in the broadest shade outside and in the middle of the house with all apertures open, it became somewhat tolerable. The clouds in the Northwest were wind-rifted and draggling To-wards eight P. M. the heavy bank that had settled

due North commenced to show signs of disturbance.
In an hour or more sheet lightning played more or
less vividly behind it, and by midnight a short tolerably gusty wind swept about us, rousing light
sleepers and rattling doors and casements annoy-
ingly.

Curious too, for the past two nights, I have noted
a large section of an arc of dimly radiating twilight,
directly on the horizon under the North Pole Star.
It looked like the reflection, tho' moving, from a
quarter-moon or rather distinct Aurora. Was it pos-
sibly the summer solstice apparition of the borealis?
It surely must have been; for these premonitions
evidence an electrical storm, whose seat natural phil-
osophists have come to conclude resides at the North
Pole. Or, if not, what could probably throw the
long evening twilight, reflected often in the Northeast, so far due North, at half-past ten or a quarter
to eleven o'clock at night? At eight, some twenty
or thirty minutes after sunset yesterday, we enjoyed
that as rare phenomenon of the after-rays of twilight stretching clear across the zenith and down to
within 25 or 30 degrees of the opposite horizon. It
formed broad, then tapering and expanding, belts of
whitish light in concentric or eliptic lines from
Northwest to Southeast, a clearly defined amphi-
theatric series of alternate white and blue bows. It
was not so discernible in the Southwest.

This morning, July 2d, at ten minutes after three
A. M. I saw the time on my watch dial by daylight.
Tho' one could stand a blanket on him at midnight, at 9.30 A. M., as I was returning from Church
carrying a chalice and paten, the reflection of the

sun on the paten burnt my chin; and people are
sitting around in the open air getting what coolness
their ingenuity can eke out of the pretty constant
breeze from the South, by a few points East. We'll
have a crack and blow yet, and I doubt very considerably if somebody or bodies have not had one or
the other or both lately, no great distance from here.

July 3d.—We have not had it yet, tho' the wind
has now veered around to the Northwest and the
sun again sank in clouds after a quite sultry middle
day. I learned to-day that the degree in St. Paul,
Sunday, was even 100—higher, as above stated, than
at any other point at the given time anywhere in
the United States, not excepting New Orleans.

HEAVY HUNT AND WHIMSICAL FISH.

Our sportsman and man-of-all work, to-day, con-
tends that he not only killed forty birds with forty-
one shots, but in some six weeks killed for a firm in
Tracy, twenty-four miles north, five hundred and
twenty chickens, twenty odd per day for six days in
the week! But if he did, and it is possible, he
knows more about hunting than fishing for pickerel,
mud cats and bass. He showed me a case of
hooks, artificial flies and baits, from the finest trout
hook to the great clumsy harpoon with peacock
feathers at its heel; and was explaining to me how
splendid they would be to troll with in the lake. I
am not sure but he tried his luck with some of his
flies, where no one could observe him, but one thing
was sure, he never brought back any fish. He
hooted at our coarse hemp lines and three hooks and
spoons, ordinarily used to troll for pickerel.

"Hoot, man! why sure, in Ireland if ye put out such a line as that—why it's a regular cable!—you'd be booted for scaring all the fish away. Try some of these fine flies."

"Oh! well," he was answered, "that's the difference between America and Ireland. You would have as much use for your horse hairs and silk lines here as you would for a horse's tail or a silk dress." But he insisted he was right, until I found out he was disputing in order to have a pretext for not rowing for me, so I had finally to shut him up by bidding him keep his tongue and row up. I acknowledge it was tough work in and out the many turns of the sedgy and weeded inlet; and the poor fellow was tired enough when we had caught a string of some half dozen pickerel in the old-fashioned way. In the talk by the way home he told me some curiosities anent the hawks and merlins noble folk yet use on the hunt in the old country: "When out, they 'hunt' four or five birds apiece; but when the hawks get their fill of the hearts and tidbits of their prey, they'll stop hunting, short off. Why, sir, I've shot at a bird, a snipe or grouse, and missed him; and a merlin 'd swoop down and clutch him before he'd touch ground sir! They'll jump down on a hare and clinch him with one claw on his neck and the other on his back, in a jiffy."

"Ho! talking about hunting, a man from Tracy sent me word about training a dog for him, and when I charged him $25 for it, I thought he'd let me alone. But behold ye, he sends me two, but they're not much account." And I did see the dogs about—a scabby brace—and hear he was paid, or was to be paid, $25 for each one.

July 4th.—Our part of the storm, gathering for
two days, has come. Last night at two o'clock we
were all awakened at the presbytery by the vivid
lightning in the Northwest and the sharp detona-
tions. The surplus electricity was well eliminated
by a good twenty minutes' cannonading, tho' I did
not take it that the crash was so great or the rever-
berations so earth-shaking as with us further South,
among hills and in cities. The nearest bolts measured four seconds after the flash.

The great heat wave is passing South and East;
the temperature to-day allowing one a drive out in
a fall surtout, and mildening at this, four A. M. to a
dampish coolness that is agreeable. I should guess
the thermometer had not passed 60 degrees, and that
only for an hour or two. We shall now revert to
our cool summer weather; warmth prevailing, tem-
pered by an all but incessant breeze. But these
extremes are felt by visitors much more sensibly
than by those more accustomed to them.

We have had limitless sport over the squabbles
between the

Village Worthies

in and those out of office—the all important office of
trustees of the municipality. It is about the matter,
just now, of allowing the Nuns to extend their lines
down to the lake border by vacating or not vacating
an intervening street. The feeling of the outsiders
seems in favor of conceding the Nuns the whole
property, street and all, with the portion of a hundred trees in the plantation dignified by the name of
"park"—more properly a nursery. The village

fathers insist that the street must not be touched,
because it would block out a party or two from the
other side of the railroad-cut from getting to church;
and because it would spoil the future drive along the
lake shore; and because—well, several more potent
and sapient *becauses*. Ah! and the Sisters could
have an under-bridge gangway for private entrance
secured by decree of the town government, etc.
The out-politicians put forth patriotic resolutions
what they will do when they get back into office:
one saying he will expend $100 but what the Sisters
shall have the whole property undivided; another,
this our man: "All the art of a gardener could not
make the park conceded available for private use if
the street be left"—and wanting to know in the
next breath what plan I would suggest for landscape-
gardening a plat as large as a calf-paddock.

More stories for the soldiers and marines about
our hunter, Nimrod the XXII, averring on his honor
as a man, that out of twenty-two birds in a flock he
laid about him until he knocked nineteen and hadn't
time to put his hand on a bird until he had all but
exterminated the whole covey!

FOURTH OF JULY — INDEPENDENCE DAY AT FULDA, MINNESOTA.

The unfavorable outset of the morning dampened
the patriotism of many whose clothes it but slightly
moistened, in the rare celebration of the Fourth at
Fulda. I hardly imagine the sunrise cannon shot,
which was to have been the harbinger of the day
for the forenoon performances, to have been very
sure of being carried out. Sure it is, that almost the

whole programme for the first half of the day was
dispensed with, except the march of the fifty odd
men who rode out in cavalcade to meet Rt. Rev.
Dr. Ireland; and then the disposition of the dinner
where it would do the most good, at meridian.
Some cannonading and shooting-crackering was the
voicing of the outburst of patriotism of the noisier
populace. That cannon, if but small arms, made a
grand racket withal. The procession in town was
not an imposing improvisation, for lack principally
of participants, who, all counted, could muster but a
baker's half-dozen of vehicles. It was vanguarded
by a small calibre brass band, somewhat mixed in
its composition by the control of the tenor being
thrown upon a single clarionet. The piping effect
of the small orchestra under the broad canopy of a
prairie sky was not agreeably relieved by the solitary
bycycler running out as on parade with a ten cent
child's trumpet, at which he would take a solemn
"ta-ta-taw, ah!" at every presentation of front to the
line of procession.

At the order of a sub-marshal, the crowd of men
and small boys, numbering a score and a half, strag-
gled on behind the wagons and buggies, but in a
confused tho' quiet rout. Through all these and
similar drawbacks, however, the dignified but hearty
participation of the Bishop of the Church in this
civic celebration healed many deficiencies—in fact,
at last made the day a striking success. There was
taught thereby the proper appreciation of "the glory
of the liberty of the children of God" in this country,
if it be not perfect; and it showed how highly bene-
ficial is the visible effect of bringing out the people

en masse to do honor to religion in its **chief repre-**
sentative, and in allying love of country and virtue
in a common bond. Of many things desirable this
is strikingly so—that the children of the Church
should mingle, as far as compatible with their faith
and socially, with the children of men, and thus **in**
all lawful degrees draw them to a reverence for
earth-blessing and heaven-gaining faith by public
exhibitions of the alliance and compatibility of true
love for fatherland/ here and hereafter. If the vivifying religious sap permeate not the pores and chan-
nels of the tree of public life, the juices of earth will
not nourish at the root what the sun of the skies
fails to enliven and the rain of heaven to freshen.
That beautiful continued metaphor of Romans (XI:
16, 24) would also teach that the Church is the true
Olive Tree, rooted, branched, fruitful—the world
that is even convertible, but the wild olive branches
grafted or graftable upon her. And if even the
Church show defects in individual branches, on her
human side, her root is sound, incorruptible and un-
improvable by the insertion of forced growths.

Whatever was calculated to stimulate a stran-
ger's risibles was soon over, and the stately figure
of the Rt. Rev. John Ireland, orator of the occasion, with his well-worded address of effective
Christian patriotism, gave another turn to the day.
The towns people had fitted up a large open booth,
floored, seated, **roofed** and somewhat decorated in
the body with garlands and festoons of leaves.
Some mottoes of "Liberty," "Welcome," "The
Fourth," in fancy lettering, and a brace of bouquets
graced the speaker's stand and the organ in front—

the former occupied by notables, ecclesiastic and
lay, the latter environed by its bevy of girls and
ladies and a triplet of male singers.   Songs and band
pieces introduced the exercises, while the open-air
hall was filling, and the long space under either eave
was being enlivened with busts of men and boys—
sturdy farmers and lads, brawny mechanics, farm
people, huddled groups.

The grand, simple and simply sublime "Declara-
tion of Independence" being recited in an oratorical
and emphasized manner by a lawyer (new resident
of the village), and, of course, whole-souledly ap-
plauded, the presiding officer, Mr. Woolsencroft,
introduced Dr. Ireland for his oration.   Needless to
say, the eloquence of words and earnestness of manner was grounded upon great solidity and appropriateness of Christian and social matter in the address,
occupying something over an hour in its delivery.
An accommodating and skillful physician took
down the address in stenographic characters, and it
was fully expected we should have a full report *in
perpetuam rei memoriam*" for the press to copy
everywhere, citizens to frame in their homes and
hand down to their children.   Especially was it the
business of the managing committee to procure and
distribute copies among the colonists.   But after
months' delay nothing of the kind has been done,
and we must only console ourselves for the irrepa-
rable loss by the reflection that those present were
so vividly impressed by the moving eloquence and
Christian patriotism of their Bishop that they will
not only remember it to their latest day, but have
ere this repeated it so often to others that they know
its substance by heart for future repetition.   The

rest of the programme was devoted to desultory
sports, winding up with a dance at 8 P. M., and
thereafter until the "wee sma' hours." The comical
interspersion of the evening was a race against himself by that singularly prominent bycycle strider,
who must have tooted his tin trumpet lustily to
make his hind wheel catch up with his front in the
contest in which he was the sole visible competitor.
Maybe the winged Goddess of Liberty waited upon
him and spurred him like did Minerva of old, to
add zest to the glory of the Fourth. The but seldom
rippled gravity with which he had the cheek and
jowl to blow that horn for the onset must have remained, as it certainly inaugurated, the most laugha-
ble bit of humor in all the sports.

PRAIRIE DRINKERS.

I scarcely know how many, if any, drinkers were
developed in the course of the evening after the
dignitaries left. I will not, however, conceal the
truth, that a neighboring, tho' quite small, mostly
Catholic town showed less soberness than the practically non-Catholic one of Fulda. Partially this
may be accounted for by the fact that the former
was left without controlling guidance to the unscru-
pulous fun of a small clique of half-grown boys and
fellows, whose proof of asserted manhood lay only
in the exhibition of the quantity of beer they could
gulp in an out-of-the-way grove, and the racket
they could raise, what with crackers and pistols,
what with their brazen-muzzled throats Without
going into further moralizing on the subject in hand,
it may be well to state plainly that the best colonizers are unanimous in declaring abuse of drink to be
the greatest enemy of their projects. And we find

those most engaged in planting Catholic settlements
taking a firm stand against intemperance and holding up, in general, for total abstinence as the surest
means to cut off even remote temptations from the
unwary.

An old word of Rt. Rev. Dr. Ireland comes in
place: "A Minnesota farmer must work persever-
ingly and energetically. The man who will appear
in his field when the sun is high in the sky; who
must go into the village two or three times a week,
to lounge around the railway station or the grocery
store, is sure to fail. I have met specimens of this
kind, and have heard them too often blaming the
country for the results of their own idle habits, not
to wish to meet more of them. * * * There is
no hope for those who love whisky in our colonies,
and as we have built no poor-houses they will starve
on the prairies. We do not want them." With
whom Mr. John Sweetman, his lay associate in
colonizing Murray County, is in perfect accord, in
his letter of December 15, 1883, when describing the
qualifications of a settler, especially under his revised
plan of operations: . . . "I shall conclude this by
warning off from the prairies one class—*drunkards.*

"They cannot succeed. They will surely find their
way to the nearest village, where the vilest drink is
always to be found, no matter how much it may
pretend to be a temperance town with saloons
strictly prohibited.

"I warn the families and friends of drunkards that
the prairie is the worst place for them. They will,
as I said before, at once find out where drink is to
be obtained. They will find plenty of congenial
companions who will surely show them the way to

get through their money, no matter how much it
may be."

Pity! shame! rather, that two virtues—the natural one of patriotism and religion, the epitome of
all—should be abused by being made the occasion
of treason against reason and mankind, and sacrilege
against God and faith!

July 6th.—To-day was raw, with cold north
wind so disagreeably brought home to our feelings
thro' a broken pane of glass, that a body would feel
like going to bed to get warm, as I know of some
one doing.

The show of a storm of which we had had signs
and a slight touch, I just learn, turned out a quite
serious hurricane at Graceville and on the line south.
The violent wind leveled several houses, killed a boy
outright by falling timbers, injured others pretty
badly, **and** scared the community at the Northern
colony, **if** not out of their wits, severely anyway.
A wind storm is reported also from parts of Wisconsin and Iowa on the same **day** on which we had
the fearfully blue signs here, on July 2d.

A NAMING DAY.

July 7th.—The weather has come back to its normal **summer** temperature, fair sky, cool **winds**,
brigt shine—

"And the birds make music all the day!"

And we• opened, accordingly, the Nun's pier at
"Harbor Grace," on their bit of lake shore. They
enjoyed their first boat ride, with our Cuban, Marie
Laine, gracefully guiding the rudder.

It is rather a **new-fangled kind of a sail we have**

fashioned and does not work very well, especially
in tacking—and the rudder is on a par with the two
"wings" attached to the side in lieu of a center board.
But all our company are green sailors and mind so
little the inconveniences of our old rough-plank
hulk, that they came back to "Harbor Grace" delighted. We named our fine points and bays on
Lake St. Rose to-day. The larger coppice, with
greater number of shrub trees, we call "Bird Nest,"
because the little ones sing their matins, lands, vespers and complins there, interspersing their Little
Hours thro' the long, sweet summer days. This is
thick and bushy too—fine retreat for their tiny nests
and nursery for their tender young, hid away from
the many kites and hawks. The opposite bay we
content ourselves with calling "Grove Bay," for the
quite pretentious set of cottonwoods at Mr. Rad-
ley's, across the bridge, where picnics are held and
festive youths while away sunny hours on Sundays
and off-days. But the trees are really not more than
a quarter to a half grown; and are only dignified by
the name of a grove by comparison with the lower
brush along the lake edge. The long, high promontory, on account of an arbor projected there—the
material brought, the seat already made—we named
"Arbor Point." But alas! the project came to grief;
for the carpenter who had a lumber yard discovered
the materials, and imagining they had been stolen
packed them, seat and all, away to town.

The little beach near town is denominated "Parklet Beach," for its proximity to the town park; the
low lands opposite "Arbor," "Meadows"; the turn
of the elbow-shaped point beyond the outlet, "Point
Marie." We tried to find some appropriate point

for the name of "Sharon" in honor of our **Nuns of**
the Holy Child's superb Institute near Philadelphia,
but could not succeed in pleasing ourselves. The
most beautiful spot and the nearest to being a hill
would be the fine, sloping knoll back of "Arbor
Point," in fact, including it; and some day when a
large College, for instance, or great Western Industrial School, shall have been established there,
overlooking the town and rolling prairies, the lake
and its then deeply wooded shores, we shall **come**
together and name it beautiful "Sharon Hill."

I was shown to-day a flax plant nearly two and
a half **feet** in height, already flowered and seeding.
It was proof of the push of this rich soil.

Towards **night** yesterday evening, an ugly black
waste **of clouds** poured **over the** sky from the North-
west to the Southeast, like routed, retreating cavalry,
smoking with straggling **mists of** perspiration—all
succeeding a day of **glorious** shine and fairness.
With **but two words of change, it is** the picture pre-
sented **by one of the** Shakspearean sonnets I have
been **conning these two days:**

"SUNSHINE AND CLOUD."

"Full many a glorious morning have I seen
    Flatter the (prairie wilds) with sovereign eye,
    Kissing with golden face the meadow green,
    Gilding pale (lakes) with heavenly alchemy;
    Anon, permit the basest clouds to ride
    With ugly rack on his celestial face,
    And from the forlorn world his visage hide,
    Stealing unseen to West with his disgrace."

Again this morning the picture was reversed, and the day ends with a heaven full of glorious sunset colors, bright yellow above the royal couch, like freshest sammets and corded hangings of lustrous silk. A bank and promontory in front of crimson; up sky, orange. Far over the zenith, rose and rich red, paling all until the curtains immediately above the setting glowed with last bright orange. And in the open heavens, delicate beading with exquisite blue between, and the indefinable light that is all but unearthly, calling on to the beyond.

One would be tempted to outrage astronomy by imagining the Aurora Borealis reflected some of the splendor of its fiery coloring on the burnished morn and eve, so full of fire they show. Indeed, the rise and set are both removed from their normal latitude, as compared with further south; the sun seeming to come up inside of northeast and set north of northwest—certainly due northeast and west.

CELESTIAL GLORIES.

July 9th.—How can we pass over this celestial glory without giving fit praise to the Eternal Artist, the God of Beauty! If these be but reflections from His sun's face, how much more of His own, Fount of loveliness! It was half an hour before sunset, and clear off in the southeast. Three grand mountains of clouds! Behind them the most brilliant stationary range of great shelves of rock, like precious stones from the foundations of the celestial city, wherein numberless caves recede, well defined in shaded lines of beauty.

These Titanic rosy and sapphire recesses are par-

apetted in front against the immense walls of coral
rock looming up behind and around, whose higher
receding gorges and culminating peaks are filled
and capped with heaps of vapor-snow. The white
laps of the skyey Alps throw out the deeper colors
of the rocks and mountain flanks in such enchanting
contrasts of lightsome shadings over the fairy caves,
that we cry out with exultation: "My God! how
beautiful must Thy light be to reflect such scenes to
fallen earth and mortal eyes!"

Before this heavenly background two opposing
glorious panoramas of mountain-clouds move majestically into and past one another. These proces-
sions are not illumed, rather darkish blue and shaded
to define themselves in every feature against the
background. Every shifting of the sky scenes by
the fair-weather angels call forth renewed expressions of delight. Finally, a magnificent rosy peak
of light coral ascends above the snow banks and
blue, higher and higher—bends over more than the
sculptured town of Pisa until—*mirabile dictu!* the
base gives way and the mighty eminence seems
ready to topple. It does not. It only breaks off
and floats upwards self-sustaining, like the "pillar
and base of truth," figure of the supernatural Church,
as described by the great Louis Veuillot. Under-
mined from below by the machinations of secret
societies and apostate kings and baseless upon earth,
she still stands majestic aloft, upborne by an invisi-
ble power and sustained of God.

After a half-hour the dim blue ranges float past
one another and leave the rose caves and coral reefs,
the mountain snows in the laps of the towering

Ossa-upon-Pelion, in their scarcely dimmed celes-
tialness. The god of day descends and shedding
the light of his face over all the the western firmament hides his flaming forehead behind his barred
cloud-prison. "*Et umbrae ex cacuminibus montium
. . . cadebant.*"

There are left in the opposing sky but the ghosts
of the whilom Alps—the ashes of the heavenly
burnings, smouldering, yet not consuming. The
informing lightning passes swiftly into the dull
masses, heaped like charred paper, and shoots and
quivers in ascending river-like tongues, sheeting the
now dark caves with sudden gold—flashing up beyond them into the darkening ether, blazing up in
the mountains of ashes. 'Tis a brighter glory than
that departed, because it is life from within, not a
reflection from without. Such might be the soul
after the splendors of earth are past—splendors that
are but reflected, exterior, temporal, until the informing fire of hidden grace makes the dead man
live, and the undying spirit flame but the brighter
from the ashy corpse.

CROPS AND GARDENS.

July 10th.—I saw a field of small standing oats
headed out. More grass is ready for the mower.
It is continuous and new grass harvest on the prairie
from about the first third of June, in good summers,
on till nearly the end of October. As the increasing
sun successively dries up the lower lands and in-
vades the sloughs, one by one, the new crops succeed
one another. I verily believe, and am susta'ned by
some practical farmers, that there could be three hay

harvests, taking two months each between the cut-
tings. Those prairie farmers who are raising cattle
principally make it a business to cut and press hay,
selling it to large buyers at the railroad towns or
shipping it to large cities.

I noted particularly and measured by eye some
grass and vegetation roots in a caved-in ledge of the
lake. The fibres of the roots run down below the
two-and-one-half or three-foot loam into the gravelly
dirt; the longest reached as low as four feet. And
certainly nature must make provision by putting the
roots below ordinary freezing depth, and make
allowances for the extraordinary. Here in midsummer we are eating the finest radishes. They are
firm, brittle and from as large as the ham of your
thumb to the smaller, as big as your fore or middle
finger. Lettuce is still coming on fresh, and young
onions are not run out. I ate a few strawberries
some days ago; but my particular treat of the delicacy was as remarkable for its acidity as for its
rarity. Some wild ones also have been eaten by the
Nuns and pronounced palatable. The better potatoes have blossomed, and I have heard some two
farmer's wives boast they would have new potatoes
for the Fourth of July. Maybe they did. Corn,
the best, is now about a foot high, and generally
looks thrifty.

Far-seeing people who are industrious will raise
all the vegetables they can; and the enormous quantities they can produce from even an ordinary garden plot in this soil will keep them jumping to
clear the fast growing weeds and wild grasses; but
in the end yield them all they can house for the

longer winter one may expect. This is the paradise of gardeners and root raisers.

TWIN CITY OF THE NORTH.

July 19*th.*—I have been eight days in the Northern Metropolis; and, little as I like cities as compared with the purer country, I am more and more astounded at the marvelous development of this Western New York and Brooklyn, called St. Paul and Minneapolis. Their rivalry is something on a grand scale; the differences of business they claim, severally, run into the sum of seven or eight millions in a short time, and their house building amounts to from 1,500 to 2,000 structures going up simultaneously in each place, winter and summer. The two cities combined are said to rank about third in the United States in the matter of general business; and when their but four-mile-separated suburbs join, as they are continually tending to do, the possibilities of the future Twin City at the head of Mississippi navigation, in reach of the great lakes and midway of the continent from every direction, are simply incalculable. But let some one else chronicle cities.

How glad I am to get back to my prairie with its simple beauty, its peaceful rest, its better friends— back to my letters from friends and good children.

"Oh, who would inhabit this bleak world alone!"

Yes, but some are most alone when in greatest crowds. It is my weakness, or strength. It is not so much the Thomas a Kempian reason: "The more I converse with men the less I return a man," tho' that be partially the personal truth; but modern civilization, as understood and professed practically in our business cities, is so mechanical, wooden, stony, iron. There is the eternal sameness of great dead, smoked walls and smoking roofs and filthy streets; the elbowing madness of rushing crowds; the ever anxious brow and bent body of the seeker of Mammon's favors; the horrid squalor of poverty and pinched faces beside the palatial, park-environed homes of the princes of fortune. Like the poor famishing Arab in the desert who found a bag, and hoping to Allah it were dates or figs, discovered it full of miserable baubles of pearls, one finds but machinery, hard money, man-culture, and no fountain of living waters, in the hearts of great cities. And tho' we must not judge harshly and must look below the seething surfaces of the sea of tossed mankind for the real pearls and coral caves and painted shells in its depths, still I could not refrain from apostrophizing: "Ye simply flowered prairies; ye pellucid lakes and clear-breasted waters; ye living in the grasses and rushes; soarers on high, mewing, whistling, trilling, warbling tribes; ye waving tree-lets and low shrubs, I greet ye all again and rejoice with you in the commonest, best gifts of the sweet God of Nature, blest be His name!"

SOUTHEASTERN MINNESOTA.

Going back and forth to the Mississippi along the Southern line of railroad last week, I found the prairie crops about the same as in Murray County. No corn is past plowing or "laid by." Some headed oatfields and a little headed wheat, west of Mankato.

Garden truck is in its first summer yield; a few stuck peas and beans, potatoes about all blossomed,

but some considerably bug-eaten, and scarcely any
messes of new ones. Haying is going on pretty
extensively and the yield is fair, even often abundant
on good, well-tended farms. I understand some
barley and rye is being cut, and I saw fields yellow-
ing and goldening for the sickle.

Advancing past Mankato to the East into the
wooded prairies and forty-mile belt of timber along
the Mississippi, things are considerably more advanced than on the open prairies. All the wheat
and oats are headed out and filling fast for the harvest, coming on in two or three weeks. There is
more hay and the meadows are evener and better,
tho' the grass is not so heavy as on the prairie, or as
the slough grass. Corn, in several fields, is plowing
for the last time or actually "laid by"—tho' the
greater portion seen from the track is not higher
than the prairie product; say, averaging some twenty-two to twenty-five inches. Patches, however, of
garden and field corn will reach three and one-half
or four feet, and I have heard of stalks standing six
or seven feet. As usual in our Western World,
people do not pay half attention to farm gardens,
too anxious to get at the more money-producing
crops to raise necessary vegetables for their own
consumption, not to speak of sale. Few or no gardens are apparent in smaller towns here, tho' more
in larger burgs and extensive villages. In this latter,
I saw stuck peas standing waist and breast high.
Potatoes generally are luxuriant and clean of bugs;
pretty fair cabbage and beets; lots of great undergrowth of rhubarb, currants and gooseberries. The
two last grow also wild on the prairie lakes and
yield tolerable berries.

In the vegetable markets of St. Paul, you find any quantity of fresh early vegetables, past the middle of July; young succulent onions, lettuce, strawberries, carrots, beets, cauliflower, head-big cabbage, fist-big turnips, single or double-fisted new potatoes; abundance of small flower bouquets of flesh colored roses, crimson and purple fuchsias, Sweet Williams, etc.

LAKE MINNETONKA.

July 16*th*—Our orphan's excursion from Minneapolis to-day recalls an episode of last year at this time—just the prime season to enjoy a run out to Minnetonka, the superbest lake in Southern Minnesota.

The rail route is very attractive. You rush thro' the suburbs of Minneapolis, the city of the level as compared with the more ascending St. Paul, past the fine lakes Calhoun, on the right, and the quieter, because less frequented, Harriet, and summer resorts for campers especially, on the beautiful left. Native woods line the road, and you pick, as you have a chance between stops, the wild flowers along the cuts. The country opens as you approach the vicinity of the station of Wayzata, by one direction, or the lake-town of Excelsior by another.

Up-hill and down-valley charms meet you at many turns, peculiarly reminding of the Ohio River scenery, or the less diversified valley of the Mohawk, in Central New York. The new "Belle of Minnetonka," or the great "St. Louis," comes steaming up with flags of many nations fluttering at the bulwarks. The irregular shores bend in and out, affording a variety of shifting scenes for hours', nay days', ride back and forth of the twenty odd miles traversed from navigable end to end, or the over-a-hundred miles of the circumference of the shore. Now little, then longer, pleasure crafts and tugs pass and repass like very gondolas, only more cheerful far.

How those wooded points project graceful into the lake, throwing into prominence the villas, peeping out with ornamental frieze and cornice and turrets from the foliage, perched on their blue-grass plots. Ho! another pleasure party salutes us on the right, and "hails" are exchanged between the merry-goers. These return as we go out, and leave us the "Narrows" free. Pretty narrow indeed! A row of slender piles stake off the space, just barely broad enough for the hull of our steamer. Right off there looms the grand "Lafayette" Hotel, a monstrous pile of hundreds of rooms—all outside rooms—in the curious Queen Anne style of architecture, and painted the oddest green and penitentiary brown. But it is elegantly appointed, and you may surfeit your rage for expenditure by paying five dollars a day—or even as much a meal, as was actually charged on the opening occasion.

The "St. Louis" is not so expensive, but still a large establishment. A dozen other hotels dot the shores and people the islands. A "cute" little island, with vined summer-house and trellised residence, is romantic enough for an idyl; and there it peers sheer out of the water, just broad enough to have no neighbors.

A "fish" is the order of the evening, and the ex-

pert can land his string of bass, delicate croppies,
or wall-eyed pike, and grosser pickerel. Again, as
we work our easy way back thro' the bays and
"Narrows," the resemblance to the "Beautiful River"
scenery is so marked you exclaim involuntarily, as
I heard a cultured lady do: "This is verily a section
of the Ohio Valley!" But the air is perfect, and
puts on a charm not felt elsewhere.

This 16th July, we went out excursioning with
the orphans and children on Lake Minnetonka—a
ride on its wind-blown bosom from 11 A. M. to 2 P.
M. Tho' grand it be, with fine points, harbors,
islands and promontories, as I have described it,
Minnetonka has not the ethereal beauty of the White
Bear, or even little St. Rose, or Buffalo Lake on the
prairies. And to-day, with the gale of wind making
it uncomfortable, it does not impress me as it did
last year. Captain Hill, the proprietor of the colossal Lafayette, has been working very hard to make
this a great summer resort, even going to the length
of establishing a special railroad line; and eventually,
for the rich, it will be brought to wide public notice.
It has had fewer guests this season; perhaps all the
visitors would not aggregate two hundred and fifty
or three hundred, and it takes many times these to
support the expensive and elegant establishments.

July 18th.—The Great Artist seems, to-day, to
have his colors on the pallet of the sky only in process of mixing. There is still a varying beauty in
the irregular dabs here and there of clotted whites,
creams and shaded heaps, all this neutral day. Towards twilight the skyful is tinted faintly, fairly.

On visiting the land office of C. St. P. M. and
O. R. R., we were shown by the general agent,
Mr. Drake, the grand sale of 105,000 acres, extending in alternate sections from the Murray County
line, south of Iona, on to past Adrian, Nobles County,
for $5.25 an acre, to the English syndicate of Close
Bros. A curiosity of the minor purchases by individuals are two whole sections bought by the
Protestant Archbishop of York, in England. The
sale is for cash, over $600,000, and includes every-
thing as it comes; and I happen to know from an
extended trip over the identical region, that there
are entire sections of rather hopeless sloughs, and
others of sandhills, fit perhaps for sheep grazing.
The entire purchase is about twenty miles square.
Mr. Drake informed us that in a week he expected
to close a similar sale of fifty thousand acres in Murray County, trenching on the environs of Avoca and
Fulda; $6.50 an acre will be the price. These are
some of the best wholesale trades in land made in
this or the neighboring States or Territories in a
great while; and include, as to the first in Nobles
County, the precise lands once held by the Catholic
Bureaus of Colonization, but of which never an acre
was sold.

Avoca, Midnight, July 19–20.—The full moon's
face is obscured by the drifting clouds from the
Southeast, but gives good light withal. In the North
is shown a startling display of electricity among the
banked and piled ranges of cloud-mountains, as
"Alps on Alps arise." The noiseless lightning now
blazes out into a sun, as quickly extinguished; now
flashes into rivers and darts in bolts—incessant,

changeful, lighting and going out, revealing the cloudy heights, caves, chasms. Glorious, unearthly! Great, my God, is Thy majesty! I gaze with awe— with no fear, but of a son. "Incline, O Lord, unto my aid! Lord, make haste to help me!"

This week two more spots are growing in the sun, making the number now not less than seven. Storms are predicted. On the 13th there were cyclonic winds, and twelve or thirteen electric storms in different localities from New Jersey and New Hampshire west to Montana, and from Missouri north to Canada. We are coming to pretty decided proofs that the electrical center is at the North Pole, and that the sun spots portend trouble in our air.

July 20th.—To-day will witness about our last fish. We trolled and bobbed over all the lower end of the lake the other day, and caught one miserable catfish. And we have wrought our way into the inlet thro' the growing weeds and beds of white blossoms (called *aquatica* something by botanists). and for our two hours' work brought out a single pike. Some other fishers caught two, and two others again a small string. The old-time dozens are no more.

The fields about our colony are finely advanced. Wheat is fully headed, and the ears taste of the "dough." Oats are much farther matured, and begin to whiten over the fields. Some Irish Barbary seed counts 125 to 130 oats to the stalk. Wheat heads measure, some five, some six inches. Corn is still backward in farms whose owners are not much used to it, and value it too little. Much will hardly sur-

vive the early frosts. I noticed some fine-looking
barley patches headed and flossed heavily. No
amount is raised hereabouts. I just heard of a good
field of grain ready for the machines in two weeks.

July 21st.—To-day opens with an unusual visitor—
a genuine heavy fog, that obscures the view of the
lake to even now at 8 A. M. Large drops of rain
exude from out the thick damp, and still the beemartins flit and hover; twit-twats chatter; sea-birds
cry and mew, and the cat-bird calls to merry heart
from the tangles of the bush banks. During the
obscurity let us speculate for a page on water.
Tho' I believe with my "Nature Remedy" man—
Dr. Felix Oswald, posing in the "Popular Science
Monthly" as *the* physician—in the use of water, I
would not coincide in his strong condemnation of
warm drink or hot water, for a great many chronic
sufferers. Get the water into you anyway and any-
how; it is the best of elements for recuperation and
cleansing the system, besides being absolutely necessary in some form or other to every kind of animal.
Writing for health seekers as a special class in my
interested readers, I would not deprive them of the
following thoroughly scientific resume:

THE HOT WATER TREATMENT.

"Dr. Eph. Cutter, in Gaillard's Journal, describes
the system of administering hot water, as originally
practiced by James H. Salisbury, of Philadelphia.
As this hot water treatment is receiving some attention by the public as well as the profession, the sa-
lient points are here reproduced:

The Salisbury System of Using Hot Water.—1.
The water must be hot; not cold or lukewarm.

This is to excite downward peristalsis of the alimentary canal. Cold water depresses, as it uses animal heat to bring it up to the temperature of the economy, and there is a loss of nerve force in this proceeding.

Lukewarm water excites upward peristalsis or vomiting, as is well known. By hot water is meant a temperature of 110 degrees to 115 degrees F., such as is commonly liked in the use of tea and coffee. In cases of diarrhœa the hotter the better. In cases of hemorrhages, the temperature should be at blood heat. Ice water is disallowed in all cases, sick or well.

2. *Quantity of Hot Water at a Draught.*—Dr. Salisbury first began with one-half pint of hot water, but he found it was not enough to wash out. . . . . .

3. *Times of Taking Hot Water.*—One hour to two hours before each meal, and half an hour before retiring to bed.

At first Dr. Salisbury tried the time of one hour before meals, but this was apt to be followed by vomiting. One hour to two hours allows the hot water time enough to get out of the stomach before the food enters or sleep comes, and thus avoids vomiting. Four times a day gives an amount of hot water sufficient. . . . . . Should the patient be thirsty between meals, eight ounces of hot water can be taken any time between two hours after a meal, and one hour before the next meal. This is to avoid diluting the food in the stomach with water.

4. *Mode of Taking the Hot Water.*—In drinking the hot water it should be sipped, and not drunk so fast as to distend the stomach and make it feel un-

comfortable. From fifteen to twenty minutes may
be consumed during the drinking of the hot water.

5. *The Length of Time to Continue the Use of
Hot Water.*—Six months is generally required to
wash out the liver and intestines thoroughly."

This is required in the understanding that the
treatment is used, as the basis of a cure, in a chronic
case of any kind; and when the patient will be *patient*, especially as he can suit the water to his taste,
as follows:

"6. *Additions to Hot Water.*—To make it palatable, in case it is desired, and medicate the hot water,
aromatic spirits of ammonia, clover tea blossoms,
ginger, lemon juice, sage, salt, and sulphate of magnesia are sometimes added. Where there is intense
thirst and dryness, a pinch of chloride of calcium or
nitrate of potash may be added to allay thirst and
leave a moistened film over the parched and dry
mucous membrane surfaces. When there is diarrhœa, cinnamon, ginger, and pepper may be boiled
in the water, and the quantity drunk lessened. For
constipation a teaspoonful of sulphate of magnesia
or one-half teaspoonful of taraxicum may be used in
the hot water.

7. *Amount of Liquid to be drunk at a Meal.*—Not
more than eight ounces. This is in order not to
dilute the gastric juice or wash it out prematurely,
and thus interfere with the digestive processes.

8. *The effects of drinking hot water as indicated
are* the improved feelings of the patient. The fæces
become black with bile washed down its normal
channel. This blackness of fæces lasts for more
than six months, but the intolerable fetid odor of

ordinary fæces is abated and the smell approximates
the odor of healthy infants suckling healthy-breasts;
and this shows that the ordinary nuisance of fetid
fæces is due to the want of washing out and cleansing the alimentary canal from its fermenting contents.
The urine is clear as champagne, free from deposit
on cooling, or odor, 1.015 to 1.020 specific gravity
like infant's urine. The sweat starts freely after
drinking, giving a true bath from the center of body
to periphery. The skin becomes healthy in feel and
looks. . . . ."

And if any one objects to the infusion of so much
liquid, tell him he is, like yourself, seventy-five per
cent. water. Add, hot water is almost the only safe
specific for the physical reformation of inebriates.

Regarding the purity of the water on the prairies,
it may be safely averred that the contents of rivers,
lakes and even of sloughs, are tasteless, colorless and
wholesome, for the eleven out of the twelve months
of the year. This odd month is in the end of June
and in July, being the only exceptional time when
more stationary waters show signs of impurity by
scum or bad odor, as it is the ordinarily hottest season in this latitude. There are, indeed, special localities after you leave the middle line of Minnesota
and Dakota, where you find some lakes and stagnant
river bottoms alkalined to such a degree as to require
boiling before their water can be used for drinking
or cooking.

Wells and cisterns, which are properly boxed,
(they generally call the lining with jointed pine
"curbing,") and carefully dug, either entirely above,
or far below, the blue or black clay strata, furnish
unexceptionably good water.

We do not, however, include the plains proper as distinguished from the prairies; for the latter at higher altitudes often have no escape from alkali and other bad elements except by boring the fine artesian wells.

There is the least here in summer or early autumns, of

"The melancholy days . . . . the saddest of the year."

A dash of rain and a growl of thunder dissipated the gloom in a jiffy: such in short is the sequel of the fog spell we are now thro'—all gone while I would write out these *water* pages.

How beautiful to see the heavenly prayers of the Missal verified, so frequently, to the letter, in the Convent of these good Nuns of the Holy Child Jesus, some of whom go to Holy Communion nearly every day, and all several times in the week. The celebrant so often reads prayers of the Post Communion especially referring to the family of the faithful present, who have that day participated with him of the Sweet Mysteries of the Divine Table; and alas! seldom is there one to share them with him and make true the blessings called down upon the communicants. Against one and all anyways Jansenistically inclined, one must heartily believe in frequent worthy feeding upon our Lord, "the Way, the Truth and the Life," the Viatecum of wayfarers by the Truth towards Life that is, and shall never be swallowed up in death; more notably for many

religious who share in part with the priest in the
New Law some of the ordinary privileges of the
Holy of Holies, within the sanctuary veil.

July 24th.—Our occupation for a few days has
been the plying of the trade of the Apostles in sail-
making. We have indeed but a sorry hulk of a
flat-bottomed, rough-board, lockless sort of a boat.
And we are inexperienced enough tradesmen and
sailors. Our first trial showed our ignorance of the
craft. We had no breeze, and it was perhaps a
blessing; for with our poor tackle we might have
found the nearest land, as the Irish wag suggested,
straight under us.

To-day opens fine, sunshine, clear lake, good air.
But, all of a sudden, a dense fog arises, creeps over
from the East and down from lake head, and we are
enveloped. By a quarter to eight it is lightlier, and
the sun struggles to launch thro' his glittering spears.
Some predict these fogs, if they continue, will
shorten the grain crop, which God forefend!

Two Prairie Pets.

We have caught a couple of pets lately. I got hold
of a fire-eating, full-blooded yellow-head, an irrepressible grain-preyer. He could scarcely fly a rod,
having been disabled somehow, and being young besides; but had sharp claws, snappy beak, and would
fight you as literally as he could, even in his advanced pin feathers, with tooth and nail. He has a
scolding *caw*, something like a soreheaded crow's.
Indeed he resembles the famous marauder mate-
rially, and is, like him, a great pest to corn.
They not only pick the grains. and ears, but league

with the rascally gophers—the **little** striped, short-tailed prairie squirrel—in pulling up whole acres of **young** corn sprouts.

Then, a townsman has what he calls his "canary," tied with a strong twine about **the** leg to a stake in **his** back yard. This singer's legs are all of twelve **inches** high, and he stands, in **his** brown **coat** and dun leggins, over two feet in his tight boots. He is somewhat knock-kneed, by reason of his youth and infirmities, having been left on the prairie by his unfeeling three-and-a-half foot parents to the use-lessness **of his** legs and tender wings—neither able to **locomote nor even** help himself up on his gaunt limbs when he once gets down. He is, namely, **a young** ostrich **of** these parts—an **infant** sandhill **crane** with a "peep," "peep," quite like a tiny chick. His main body is deep brown with under wings of dirty blue; his head is fuzzy, light brown, pin-feath-ered, lighted by an **eye** perfectly round, of beautiful **brown**, as large and with as distinct a pupil and iris **as a man.** His beak, with decided pecking inclina-tion, **is long** and tapering—about five inches.

We have been eating our unhoed and once-plowed potatoes for a week, and the Sisters **are** getting some sparse first fruits from their unculti-vated garden. The tubers are pestered by the bugs, **but it** is rather **late to** harm much, except perhaps in **the size of the roots.**

Very pretty wild tiger lilies (red) have been found, **and** have graced our chapel altar many mornings.

July 28th.—After several **days** busy with other matters, we resume our journal **to** note that there has been great racket—"fuss and feathers," we

might put it, if it were just that—on the railroad
these three or four days. The train has been bringing back six, eight and more empty cars from a spot
up north from Avoca, where a new town named
Wilson is building. Its projector is a man evicted by
his tenants, they say, in Ireland, who came over to
buy and possess a town, all his own. The railroad
needs all the paying stations it can raise to keep up
rolling stock, and pay a small surplus over running
expenses. Hadley bids fair to become a good grain
station. Slaton is pretentious enough to have fought
in its baby clothes for the assertion of its eligibility
for the county seat, and came near "lobbying" thro'.

A Well or Two.

There have been several wells dug in our township lately. It is a very simple process. The borers
erect a three-legged derrick, with block and tackle,
whence a windlass lets down an auger a foot or two
in diameter. Two men turn the auger with hand
spikes, boring down thro' the soft loam sand, and
sometimes gravel, then blue and black clay, for say,
fifteen or sixteen feet, and meet veins of water in
abundance. The depth of blue clay is as far as you
ordinarily bore; if you stir it up you are forced to
bore thro' it, often from sixteen to forty feet. It is
dry, hard, impermeable matter, stops the flow of
water, and has the reputation of spoiling the wells,
where it holds contact with the water. Wells are
dug and "curbed," that is, planked down the sides,
for eighty or ninety cents a foot. The Nuns' well
is some ninety feet deep, and has given trouble on
account of "seeps" making the water offensive.

These are two most glorious days we have just
enjoyed, sunshiny, but cool and bracing, delightfully
full of the tonic that gives vigor and health.   Such
is Minnesota's finest and peculiar weather, inspiring
these strictly descriptive verses:

MINNESOTA'S SUMMER CLIME.

Now perfect-mixt of climes,
   Of all that sweeten air or earth bedeck,
Thy crispy summer times
   Thine angel saved from Eden's wreck.

As is thy sheen of stars
   From out thy depths of limpid blue;
As spring sun's glinting bars
   The earth and spirit's strength renew:

So seems it me these days
   Come down from ether's starry height,
Descending on the rays
   "Sky-tinted waters" mirror white.

In summer solstice e'en
   When burn the ardors evermore,
Sweet breath of snow, I ween,
   Thou breathest from the Arctic shore.

Wild flowers, thy frequent spring—
   Thy soil, quick fruits and later, yields:
Lands, lakes invite the wing
   Of birds and men to quickening fields.

To sanitarium, thee,
   From genial clime and country come
Strong, sick, the bond and free,
   Wealth-seeking—refuge, health and home!

TAYLOR'S FALLS ON THE ST. CROIX.

Not far from as lovely a day as this, tho' vastly
hotter, was it last summer, when a party of four of

us crossed the lake-river at Stillwater, Minnesota, and passing over to Hudson, on a primitive flat of a steam ferry, steamed up the St. Croix River to the famous Dalles, or Taylor's Falls. Next time, however, we beg to have better transport than afforded by that poor little steam-run concern, called by courtesy a pleasure boat.

The St. Croix here is a narrow strip of water, rather on the order of a series of ponds, so very shallow in places we had to tack every fashion to get the junk ahead. On one stretch we called up all hands and actually poled our way for some rods; and when we came to the great log boom (this being the ordinary channel for logging from the contiguous forests of Minnesota and Wisconsin) we were checked completely and forced to halt until word could be got by skiff to stop the booming, or "boom-up," as the technicals say. Finally, with the sun driving us from one side of the slender craft, we sweated our way up, and were well rewarded by the fresher mountain-like air breathed thro' the Dalles, and by the sight of the finest rock scenery of perhaps both States. The singularity of rougher, rockier sections in the midst of the plains and prairies, rolling for hundreds on hundreds of miles on either side, makes the Dalles more interesting features of landscape. How the word "Dalles," meaning flat or table rock, came to be applied to these great gorges of piled walls, is hard to conjecture; except that, perhaps, it refers to the actual building of the masses, seemingly in horizontal lines and as if piled one flat surface on another in the manner somewhat of human constructions. There are up-

wards of five miles of more or less elevated sites and
shapes, the "Devil," as usual in the rather profanely
famous West, getting more than his share of prominence by standing sponsor for rocks, chairs, bowls
and slides.

Here you see a great bend in the rapid Falls, en-
walled by sheer precipices rising boldly and irregu-
larly on both shores: now forming a grand Giant-
causeway front, now breaking into large points and
minor peaks. Across the falls, between the two
embryo towns, both finely situated and embowered
in stately trees and evergreens, spans an arching
bridge, setting off the natural scenery to an unusual
degree. Bridges are always beautiful, whatever it is
that consitutes the quality; but in wild gorges like
these nothing satisfies the sensation-nerve of the
beautiful so fully.

Down in the Dalles fishing smacks row to and fro
in the eddying waters; and far down, the musical
echo brings back, perfected in Nature's grand organ,
the shouted song and whistle, the forced exploding
laughter and "yodel." We climbed the rugged
roads above the Minnesota town and explored the
vicinage with cautious foot and rapid eye. No easy
task! The brushing underwood is massy and the
steeps made for goats or acrobats. Strange! we
found, as it were, great bored cisterns, as circular as
if done by human machinery, but evidently worn so
by eddying pools, carrying, doubtless, granite and
flint bowlders, for centuries of fret. One exceeded
the other in singular imitation of human craft, and
we lingered examining them.

Once out on the rocks overlooking the lower Falls,

we enjoyed a view worth double our toil and moil. The river, clear as all mountain streams are clear, wound down between the Nature-built walls of fine browned and mossed rock; the banks now lowering, now rising in beauteous change. We shouted and sang to the Echo; and the Echo talked long and sweetly back, ever agreeing to all our moods.

But what a night we passed at the hotel in the poor quarters assigned us directly under a mansard roof, heated during the day to past boiling point! At least it made us boil and froth over with the lathers of perspiration it cooked out of us, especially some rather portly ecclesiastics, whose stock in trade of entertainment amounted to doleful groans over the sultry heat, interspersed with frequent moppings. I happen to know even one spare body who deserted his bed for the hall, and steamed there as if afire.

Avoca, July 29th.—I have heard of barley and rye being harvested in the past week, some of extraordinary growth. Garden corn is tasseled in localities. This morning, the park-garden's corn (hardly more than voluntary) is tasseling at less than three feet; tho' the stalks look thick and healthy, barring that the leaves are too close. A few stands are silking.

The weather has been varying; for two weeks cool, but warm, even sultry, after dinner for a short time, breeding some night musquitoes. Yesterday was rather cold. To-day is bright and sweet, with good northwest breeze.

On St. Anne's eve we trimmed and set our sail
boat, launching her under the name of the feast,
"Santa Anna." The wind was north by a little
west, and we had to pull over with oars to the
north shore in order to get a start. We cruised a
half mile at a brisk run. We spied a batch of wild
ducks on the upper lake, perhaps some five dozen.
Good omen for opening of the season on August 15.
A few will kill game in the closed time, but they
get little good out of it; as breeding fowl are strong
of flavor and lean, they are quite unfit to eat.

A Run into Dakota and Iowa,

BEFORE we detail the account of the Six Weeks in the Mountains, we find this a suitable intervening space for a more general description of a ten days' run into Dakota and Iowa at about this season last year.

The old story is often yet a stern reality about parties inscribing on their canvas-covered wagon on the tramp for Dakota, "Dakota or *Bust*," and coming back with "Dakota" heavily marked out and "Busted, by Gum!" inserted in its place. But it hardly applied to us in the early fall of '82, when we two gentlemen of leisure made a trip into a tract roughly estimated at four hundred by four hundred miles square, now before Congress as a candidate for admission as a State. We had seen an exhibition of Dakota's products, natural and cultivated, funny rocks and bowlders, geodes and crystals from the "Bad Lands," and its stupendously large, nay overgrown, squashes, roots, grains, and weeds. These were kinds of things that could not be manufactured like wooden hams and nutmegs from the land of inventions and humbuggery, æsthetic culture and some pure *cussedness*. Neither could they well be duplicated this side of California or the Gulf States.

But it is better to see, for one's self, even if only representative portions of the enormous territory could be visited.

"Would a little trip of five hundred miles suffice, and that in a circle around the contiguous corners of Minnesota, Iowa, Nebraska and Dakota!" Hardly—maybe! We would go into the country of "magnificent distances" indeed: for five hundred miles can be covered here by putting down the point of·your finger into the intersection of the four States on the ordinary map.

It is August and all is in freshest bloom. From Heron Lake, Minnesota, to Flandreau, Dakota, was all old stamping ground; and we could find few accessions to our wonted observations.

FLANDREAU, DAKOTA.

Flandreau, a prairie town of some pretensions, is named after an old French settler, and a Catholic, no doubt, who drove a stake and threw up a tent here some two decades or more past. It was then the land of the Dakota Indian, and a man's scalp wasn't worth hardly as much as a good powdered wig—until the scalp could be dressed. The Pipestone Reservation is not far off now, and a curious body may run over and witness a cheap savage pageant of a war dance, some Indian drunkenness and slovenliness, a little sharp-shooting, and mayhap an old-time arrow shot, for a few dimes' admittance. Sometimes, tho', they advertise to show, and do not follow up the programme. So all one gets for his trouble is the sight of some ragged old tents propped on a rough, pyramidal-shaped frame of poles, a set of squaws, squatting about making baskets and canoes of birchwood for trinkets to sell; a lounging brave or two, much the worse for wear, and with nothing remarkable about them except the way they wear their new-fangled, civilized suits, and the way they do not wear their hats on their unkempt poles. A few half-breed children, a bright-eyed Indian lad or lass rolling lazily about and talking baby-talk, fills the picture—if you throw in a wrinkled old squaw, a battered, blinking, blear-eyed, aged horse thief; and take in the whole culinary department, by adding some strings of jerked meat, a few pounds of bacon, and a hodge-podge pot simmering over a fire on a pole crossed on forked stakes.

But we came to see white people; and to say that we saw crowds of them in every town of any size down the road and valley of the Sioux River to Yankton, would scarcely express the very truth. People? Why you might go into some thoroughfares of New York and New Orleans and you would not meet with more persons in a given time than in Sioux Falls, Sioux City and Yankton. Fairs were going on all along the line, and all the world was abroad; and all the hotels, hostelries and boarding houses so full you did well to secure a camp bed in the "office" or waiting room.

About Flandreau are the wide, slightly rolling prairies, yet full of game at a reasonable distance, and fragrant with wild flowers. We visited no particular farms; but one can easily take for granted that anybody with the least Western "get up" about him can raise what he pleases in this grand, sandy loam, except, perhaps for a while, fruits like pears or peaches. It is almost useless to repeat that all the Western prairies, outside of strangely rock-

dotted portions and surprising Dalles about unex-
pected river torrents, are all of about the same
identical formation as to quality and, no doubt,
also as to chemical combinations of earth.

Sioux Valley.

Descending South until you touch the Sioux River,
you come into one of the simply most charming
wooded and watered stretches of rolling prairie.
The modest Sioux increases in width and volume as
you go down, and its banks are profusely fringed
with goodly timber; in places, thick shrubbery.
Towns, great and small, succeed one another as
rapidly as one would imagine they must in this
favored valley. "Picturesque as the valley of the
Mohawk," would be the natural expression of a
comparer, minus the more cultivated state of the soil
and the frequency of well-ordered farm establishments of the famous Central New York vale. But
the fine Sioux meanders just like its counterpart; the
railroad follows its banks as closely; bursts of
glorious landscape of land and water delight as
frequently, and with more wild freshness and un-
touchedness. The glint of the sun on wave and leaf
is purer, the air lighter and sweeter, the sky limpid. Oh! for more inhabitants for these glorious
sites for homes away from cities, "confusion worse
confounded"; for Catholic spires and school bel-
fries to rear amid these shades of peace; sweet-faced
nuns to pace and bright-eyed youth to romp in
these natural avenues; and the beaming face of a

happy priest to foster all God's work for soul and
earth! But she is coming, Holy Religion, and
taking up her seat in spots wide apart, collecting
her scattered children, and not forgetting the building of their happy homes on earth, while she turns
the gaze and inner heart to the everlasting abodes.

The church at Flandreau we found on the suburbs, just only closed in and made serviceable for
summer use; no altar but a rude frame, no plaster
nor laths, benches of rough boards. It will make a
handsome structure when finished, and the high-
ceilinged interior with semi-circular apse for the
sanctuary, and outside a tolerable belfry, combine to
promise a good-looking church.

SIOUX FALLS

is a much more pretentious and more beautifully
sited town or young city than its northern neighbor. It is a young queen of the hills, as you
would call its more than usually high-rolling streets
and environs. Its streets are well laid out, and
green with lines of maples, cottonwoods and harder
trees. Buildings and stores are tasty and some
even elegant. Church spires crown well-planned
and executed houses of worship, especially of the
Protestant denominations. The sweet Sioux rolls
past and thro' in a somewhat rougher bed and
between high banks, refreshing, re-greening and
enlivening earth and gladding man and beast.

A fair was going on, and we must not miss the
opportunity to see the animals and products which
the country could show. It was its first fair, and
the ground was situated in a luxuriant corn field

with many of the stalks standing. The ring indeed
was not much of a novelty and the animal exhibit
was small. One notices the paucity of horses and
draught animals out West, and wonders why some
less western and *southern* States, which raise horses
and mules in such abundance, do not furnish men
with brains and capital to make a great trade in this
line, and thus be a source of mutual benefit to both
sides of the valley of the Mississippi. Vegetables
and ground products, however, were plentiful, and
showed prolific soil and some care of culture.

On down the line of railroad we passed into more
and more beautiful regions, some of whose inhabitants have had the sensible poetry to name after
the primeval garden they must resemble. We are
not astonished to hail a representative Paradise and
an Eden. Little Eden! how beautiful in name
and truth. It is however off the line of Dakota and
just over the borders of Iowa.

Ha! but we had our own private chuckle at the
grave conductor, who got us off our track in his
comfortable enough freight caboose and took us a
pleasant jaunt over the borders and back for—just
nothing.

"Lookee, here, I want fare for this trip!"

"Very likely," we returned; "but you won't get
it. We bargained to go on in Dakota and you have
lugged us off into Iowa, and you may quietly get us
back on our route."

"Yes, but you've got to pay for it."

"Not a red, my uniformless official."

And he, after seeing he was caught, took the
matter with good enough grace and rolled us on to

the land of promise, Eden. We had some adventure there; a big hunt before dark that day and some chickens of our own killing for supper, late enough to make us render justice to our appetite and the cook's art.

We met some strolling blind fiddlers in the little beautiful burg, and helped them by gratifying ourselves with really charming music. They were sharp enough to get their audience *in* for a gratis concert and not let them *out* without a handsome contribution.

Next morning, another hunt and long, long ride in the fresh of the day, the grasses all dank and glistening with dew; the slight misty haziness but glorifying the atmosphere; chickens "flushing" up out of the meadow lands and snipe from the low lands.

These are but sample towns and townlets along both sides of the Sioux River as it wends its generally straight course directly south towards the great Jim River and the mightier Missouri. As intimated, all this region is well timbered—along the banks of streams peculiarly. As however you approach the junction of the three great rivers between Sioux City, Iowa, and Yankton (the now disputed capital of Dakota), the lands become lower, show signs of periodical deluges and are more specially adapted for grand meadows of prairie grass, where millions of tons of hay stand stacked, like dotting wigwams, as far as the eye can reach in every direction.

YANKTON,

a usual passing point for emigrants and supplies for all the interior from the South, is too well known for special description or more than transitory reference. Its site is more diversified with rise and fall in levels than the surrounding country. It has a small stream or two running thro' its suburbs and unusually copious fountains of water, some minerally impregnated.

The late seat of the vicariate of Dakota, removed in January, 1884, to the more central Jamestown, ruled by the famous and laborious Benedictine, Rt. Rev. Dr. Martin Marty, Yankton is better supplied with churches and schools than any point west to the Rockies, tho' this is not saying much, as there are not four other large towns. It is well known that the former abbot of St. Meinrad's in Indiana has literally made all the churches and establishments of the immense territory, which now circumscribes the Vicariate. The establishment of Bishop Brondel in wide Montana, has only divided the immense former Vicariate of Nebraska. Going and coming for years among whites and Indians, the monastic Bishop Marty has been wearing his life away for the life and weal of his fellowman; and he is still in vigor to prosecute his work. The academy established formerly at Yankton had to be discontinued, and only day schools furnish education for the growing Catholic community of whites — the Indians having a few government-supported and industrial schools.

NORTHERN IOWA.

On our return to Sioux City, we were astounded to find such a wide-awake and stirring place, away from what many would call the currents of com-

merce. Streets crowded, hotels full, brisk business
and cosmopolitan population, are outlines that faintly
describe this, but a few years ago, border town.

Then we hurried on thro' the great hay-making
portions of Iowa. The more northern counties are
beautiful gardens and farms, raising corn and grain in
rivalry of the compeer State just over the Mississippi.
Such miles and scores of miles of haying fields:
such illimitable reaches of maize, surrounding rich
farmers' residences and pouring gold into the lap of
of the State! This northwestern half of Iowa, with
all its wealth of rich prairie, is not so thickly settled,
nor perhaps so adapted to general farming and pro-
digious corn raising as the corresponding eastern
half. Along the Mississippi we have noted the
models of thrifty towns and growing cities engaged
in milling, and specially in the great lumber trade,
situated as they are on the main artery of some of
the most extensive pineries of the continent. But
back of these roll continuous hundreds, thousands,
of square miles of the choice prairies, adapted to
anything in the growing line according to their
latitude.

It is plain, however, that corn is the staple, and far
outstrips in quantity, luxuriance and profit, any other
grain. Man never put his eyes on finer fields than
those lining the almost entire route from Albert Lea
in Minnesota, in a southeasterly course, to the crossing of the Mississippi at Rock Island, Illinois. No
one need be told this whole region is long ago
"taken up," and is not being relinquished for what is
esteemed better, like corresponding Northern and
Middle Illinois.

SIOUX CITY, IOWA, Monday, July 30, 1883.

A FEW of our religious, and our Cuban, Marie, formed my company on setting out at 11.30 P. M. from Heron Lake, Minn., to Lincoln, Nebraska. We were treated to the best, tho' weak, manifestation we had yet enjoyed of the Northern Lights, on the route from Avoca to the junction at Heron Lake. It consisted of, at first, a glow of whitish light arching low on the horizon, and now and then expanding by division into long rays like departing twilight, all pointing up very similar to one's fingers outstretched apart. The diminishing points reached nearly half way to the zenith. But all was so pale, we agreed in calling it the "ghost of the Aurora."

The lands in the valley of the Missouri on the Iowa side from below Sioux City to Omaha are nearly flat, as if used to being overflowed. Swampy places occur now and then. About half the corn is large and tasseled; the other half low, and a number of fields are neglected and turned out to weeds and grass. Barley and rye are being harvested. The reserve banks of the river—provided by nature against the great overflows—stand far out from the actual water course, leaving long and wide meadow lands of great value for grazing and hay.

COUNCIL BLUFFS AND OMAHA.

Tuesday.—Very slow officials and little accom-

modations for strangers seem the order of the day
at Council Bluffs—quite a miserable-looking, muddy
place. We got trapped for an hour's delay, but
the railroad-run hotel, which makes it a business
to force custom by retarding passengers, got none of
our cash—plenty of round abuse, in lieu. It seems
the railroad companies run the dummy connection
between the two towns, and either care nothing for,
or purposely work against, travelers catching trains
on the opposite side of the river. It was, at least,
our experience both times we passed by the twin
cities here. The banks of the Missouri, the water,
and all its surroundings, impressed us as ugly and
unhealthy-looking. Large round iron pillars support the singular bridge, trestled off to a considerable distance on either of the low sand banks. There
is no provision for communication other than by
rail. Back of Omaha, and in the corporation, is
quite rolling prairie, very worrisome to teamsters
inside the city limits, but that more picturesque.
The Catholic institutions are perched around on
commanding eminences—a similar spot being reserved for the new cathedral when it shall be built.
Tho' this be all prairie land for hundreds of miles,
we found a rock quarry on the route to Lincoln.
There are doubtless others. The environs of Omaha
and all along the sloping hills of the wide, shallow
Platte River in the direction of Lincoln are well
wooded. Corn is tasseled, but a good portion we
see is low and uncultivated—a few fields of barley being cut.

There is a curious salt river in the neighborhood
of Lincoln, along which the vegetation is stunted

or killed out. But freaks of nature increase upon you as you advance into our wondrous Rockies— the home of the grand and the awful, as of the weird and novel.

ITEMS GENERAL ON PRAIRIE LANDS.

Mr. E. V. Smalley, author of "Travels" and of the "History of the North Pacific Railroad," in the "Century" of February, 1883, writes that to the west of the Missouri and in Yellowstone Park the soil "abounds in lignite deposits; tho' the whole region between the Minnesota prairies (and on the same line south) and the Rocky Mountains is (now) bare of timber. The strips . . . along water courses in Dakota . . . consist mainly of cottonwood, soft maple and alder—of no value as building material. West of the Missouri there is . . . nothing worth sawing . . . as far as the advanced spurs of the Rockies, and . . . on to the Yellow Mountains. In the gorges there is sufficient bull pine and spruce for ties and bridge timbers. . . . It is a mistake (to think) . . . that the rigorous Minnesota winter climate continues . . . all the way to the Rocky Mountains. Dakota winters are even more severe . . . because there are no forests to break the force of the blizzards. West of the Missouri the mean winter temperature steadily increases . .. and in December, January and February, in the valley of the Yellowstone, it is not ruder than in Maryland or Southern Ohio."

THE UNION AND NORTHERN PACIFIC ROUTES.

"The snow fall is much less than in the belt of country along the Union Pacific R. R. . . . There is

no serious obstacle to regular winter traffic between
Lake Superior and Puget Sound!"

One would be inclined to criticise these two last
assertions, as the partial statement of a paid agent of
the Northern Pacific R. R. The late collapse of the
work on the Canadian Pacific, on account of finding
no passable mountain gap in the route, may be taken
as a fair warning by the North Pacific, which is not
so far south of its parallel neighbor.

Rev. S. Byrne, writes: "The Northern Pacific
crosses the Territory from East to West. It follows
the Yellowstone River for about three hundred
miles, then turns North, and after having crossed a
range of mountains, soon enters into the valley of
the Missouri. It then makes its way to Helena, and
a few miles beyond that city begins to cross the
Rocky Mountains. It is impossible fully to describe
their wonderful work in a brief space, and the reader
of these lines is referred to other recent works on
the subject. There are eight hundred and forty-eight
miles of their road in Montana, and branch lines are
already commenced. The branch leading to the
Yellowstone Park will be finished in a year or less.
Besides the Northern Pacific, a branch of the Union
Pacific Railroad has been in course of operation two
years, from Ogden, in Utah Territory, into Montana.
Its great utility is widely felt; and it will be a salu-
tary stay upon the first-named road in the matter of
regulating freight and passenger rates."

"That Montana," continues Smalley, "formed the
great buffalo range and is fast becoming a vast
cattle range, verifies the assertions regarding light
snowfalls ... ," which often melt, I have learned

from another source, on short notice. North of Benton, in a large valley, the snow is melted by a periodical warm wind, and in another locality in Wyoming the railroad was blocked by herds of antelopes frequenting such a spot This may be the case elsewhere. Again says Smalley: "The forty-fifth parallel is the proposed line of division of North and South Dakota.... Montana is larger than Dakota but contains less farming land ; and, save in a few valleys, will not support a dense population. East Montana is mainly grazing; the west, a mass of mountain ridges, between which are narrow fertile valleys, where agriculture may be made profitable, but cannot be carried on except by irrigation.. .."

Again I quote Fr. Byrne: "Another and perhaps a clearer description is as follows : This territory, in its physical conformation, is naturally divided into four sections. First, the northwestern section lying between the Rocky and Bitter Root Mountains, which is very rugged and broken, and intersected by many mountain spurs. Secondly, the northern district, extending three hundred and fifty miles along the Missouri and Milk Rivers, is a vast, open plain, almost destitute of trees, and descending towards the East at the rate of five feet to the mile. Thirdly, the southeastern section, bordering on Dakota on the east and Wyoming on the south, is more rolling and better wooded. Fourthly, the southwestern section, containing fifteen thousand square miles, is very similar to its neighboring district of the Northwest where we began, that is to say, very mountainous and covered with dense forests. Several mountain peaks attain a height of over ten thousand feet."

That irrigation is going to be undertaken and pursued to some practical advantage by the General Government on a vast scale, all along the rainless regions leading up to the mountains, is confirmed by the fact that a number of artesian wells are already bored. Mr. John Fitzgerald, of Lincoln, Nebraska, a public-spirited gentleman in every sphere of business and enterprise, especially in carrying out railroad plans in the West, asserted to me that it was understood the Federal authorities would further the interests of the West by subsidies reaching still more generally among already established communities, in the matter of water supply.

LINCOLN, NEBRASKA.

To descend now from these generalities to particulars of our special journey thro' Eastern Nebraska, the name of the princely railroad contractor and banker, Mr. Jno. Fitzgerald, would suggest some attempted description of Lincoln and the flower of the settled communities in the charming southeastern portion of the State. The subject is very tempting to the delighted visitor; for than the city of Lincoln one can meet no finer city or more faultless surroundings in a long trip West. New as all things are new in this region, Lincoln is so situated on a slightly rolling and wooded prairie, that its streets are just enough varied by gentle rises and falls to cause no hardship to driving, and to be brought, withal, from the monotony of a dead level. Its buildings and business houses are not the blank, bare walls you see in similar centers of brisk trade; and the suburbs contain some of the kingliest residences, with grand yards and drives, bordered and diversified with shrubbery, plats of grass and beds of flowers. The **genial climate** is favorable **to** all growths from the daisy to the sturdy oak. **Nearly** on the utmost boundaries of the corporation **is** situated the

NEW CONVENT

of the Nuns of the Holy Child Jesus, under the prudent management of the first Superioress, Mother Agatha. The commodious and well-arranged **three** or four story building had been put up at great **expense** by a corporation to serve as a succursal establishment to a public institution **of study; and** required but the fewest changes to make it subservient to its present and future purpose **as a first-class day, and** finally as a boarding, school. Every one knows about the Catholic West, who it was that, **under the Rt. Rev. Dr.** O'Connor, was the chief **agent** in securing this fine house and property for **the** deserving community, now making such successful headway in establishing its peculiarly well-ordered schools. It is no secret either that the same great-hearted gentleman has used his deserved wealth in settling the community and constituting himself the first prop of this establishment. Needless to say, the good Nuns have so many scholars they can receive no more.

A big blackberry crop is coming on, for which low lands are peculiarly adapted: and as for fruit, Nebraska boasts of having produced the premium apples at the Exposition of 1876. I should think this somewhat confined to the eastern third or at most half of the State—some five hundred miles long.

Thursday, Aug. 3d.—On the road from Hastings to Wyoming Territory. Here is Dorchester—five hundred inhabitants, five bins for corn, an elevator and two brick stores, which I could see from the train. Crops of oats in the vicinity are good, some fine—six or eight armsful of sheaves every eight or ten yards. Barley is splendidly luxuriant ; wheat only fair and but small lots. Corn stands tolerable, medium height—some pretty low.

Friendville—eight or nine hundred inhabitants, with dozens of railroad corn bins and an elevator for grain. The prairie here is level, about like on the line from Watseca to Chatsworth, Illinois, tho' not so flat or inclining to a swampy character. The grass we see cut with oats is neither good in quality nor stands well.

Exeter—a scattered village. There are no cuts along the railroad, tho' some snow fences.

Sutton, coming next, is on rolling prairie and has considerable cuts.

Harvard—fairly undulating town of some size. About are fields of drilled corn, and we come across a sod house or two.

This official report of the Rev. J. M. Smythe, pastor of the

CATHOLIC COLONY, GREELEY COUNTY, NEB.,

is incorporated in Mr. Wm. J. Onahan's third annual report, 1882: "The original tract of the Association

was twenty-seven thousand acres, was purchased in
1877 from the Burlington and Missouri Railroad
Company in Nebraska, and is north of the Platte
River, about one hundred and twenty-five miles
directly west of Omaha. The colony is divided into
two districts, named respectively after Bishops
Spalding and O'Connor. The population now em-
braces one hundred and seventy-five families, nearly
all Irish, although France, England, Belgium, and
even New Zealand, are represented. The first colonists had hardly money enough to buy oxen, but
now they are well-to-do. The character of the
country is rolling prairie, with uplands, valleys, and
table lands; and the soil, which is a rich, dark loam,
has an average depth of from three to twelve feet,
though vegetables have been raised in soil taken out
of wells at a depth of eighty feet. The soil will
never need manure, as by sub-soiling it will renew
itself. The colony is twenty miles from a railway,
although the Union Pacific has a line to the Black
Hills surveyed through it, which will likely be built
this summer, giving an eastern and western outlet.
Although without a railroad, the people get higher
prices for their corn than are paid in the railroad
towns, as it is said to supply the stock ranches to
the west. The stock men, instead of driving their
cattle to middle or eastern Nebraska, can now fatten
them on the ranch, and ship them direct. Greeley
county is known as the banner potato county of
Nebraska. One colonist realized $1,000 off of three
acres last season, and three others planted one acre
each, and each yielded three hundred and ninety-five
bushels. The Association has only two thousand

acres **unsold,** which it offers to colonists on eight
years' time at 6 per cent. Parties who have been
renting farms at $5 per acre, have paid $2.50 for
farms in the colony and raised better crops. The
colony is situated between two rivers, so that if there
is any rainfall in the vicinity it is benefited by it. **It**
has a natural drainage, and there being no stagnant
water, there is no malaria. There are no long
winters, and the summers are not hot, the nights in
the latter season being cool and delightful. There
has never been a case of sunstroke in that country.
The climate is phenomenally healthful, and the
people hardly know what sickness is."

The region of this Catholic colony is described as
fertile as the best, and is considered by the colonization officials as the flower lands of all they control
from Minnesota to Texas. Parties within easy reach
of them, and disinterested as far as any connection
with the sale or occupation of them is concerned,
give me very favorable reports of the contentedness
of the colonists; adding that they have never had a
failure in their past seasons, and their crops this
year are rather above the average. The land **is**
cheap and given **on easy** terms.

In one-half mile from Grand Island, the station
whence the visitor takes the railroad North for
twenty-five miles to reach the stage connecting with
the colonies—poor farming land sells for $1.25 per
acre; and in four or five miles from the city, $8 to
$20 **per acre.** The Catholic congregation here and
in the neighbood numbers some eighty-five families,
while the colony now **counts two** hundred. Taking
Nebraska as **a** whole Fr. Byrne, O. P., gives the fol-

lowing items of interest: "During a period of five years the average yield of crops per acre was as follows: Wheat, eighteen bushels; corn, thirty-five; rye, twenty-five; oats, thirty-seven; potatoes, eighty. Nebraska wheat usually brings the highest price in the St. Louis market. Cottonwood, oak, soft maple, elm and black walnut are indigenous to the soil and are found chiefly along the water courses. It is in the southwestern counties we find the best supply."

Bayard Taylor, the great American tourist and scholar, describing this country, writes as follows: "This is one of the most beautiful countries I ever looked upon. There is in it none of that weary monotony that you find in the prairies of Illinois or in the swamps of Ohio or Indiana. The wide, billowy green, dotted all over with golden islands of harvest—the hollows of dark, glittering maize—the park-like clumps of timber along the course of streams, these were materials which went to the making up of every landscape; and the eye never wearies of their sweet, harmonious, pastoral beauty."

Bayard, the tourist, recalls the funnily illustrated book of A. C. Wheeler—"Nym Crinkle" of the "New York World"—on a tour on the "Iron Trail," thro' the next lower line of railroad by way of Kansas to the Rockies. He gives an illustration of the flat, limitless, buffalo-roamed plains, only you must substitute commoner cattle for the wild bison, now, like his human counterpart, the red man, moving indefinitely west and nearly extinct. An old time railroad station indicator, a great clothing store sign with an awful hand and "one mile to t're (sic!) Railroad Station Food and Water," painted with a house

brush all over it; next, "Lots for Sale," stuck on a
slanted stake and surrounded by skulls and ribs, big-
eyed owls, and present and perspective prairie
dogs—underscored "First Farm-site Speculators!;"
a house-roof covered with hides in lieu of boards or
shingles—the body buried; "ship of the plains at
sea," viz: long lines of ancient house-like wagons
pulled by a dozen oxen or mules; "ship of the plains
in dock"—our prairie schooners backed up to the
curbs of big-as-all-outdoors warehouses and being
packed by "Greasers" and land-lubbers of the cowboy persuasion, such as you see yet frequently in
Cheyenne, Denver and in their neighbors of the
foothills; a single braced-bed wagon, ornamented
by a clothes-line string of jerked beef or rather
bison, and enlivened by the proximity of two of the
proprietors cooking their meal over a camp-fire—
mules grazing in reach : and we have something of
Nym's sketches on the plains of Kansas, which will
fit any of the plains.

Six Weeks in our Rockies:

A Diary.

DIARY OF SIX WEEKS IN OUR ROCKIES.

GRAND ISLAND, NEB., Friday, Aug. 4, 1883.

IN spite of pre-arrangements by telegraph for a sleeper at Grand Island, I found nobody up in the sleeping car, and had to help myself to some slipless pillows and stretch out on the seats. Maxwell, the first place we strike in the morning, is a primitive settlement with half a dozen dingy frames. But soon after we pass it we encounter some nine hundred or one thousand sheep pasturing along the River Platte—which we are following three hundred and fifty miles. The soil is very sandy and level. No farms or houses are to be seen, but a few "bunches" of cattle and more sheep in the space between us and the interminable low ranges of mound-like hills on either hand. We encounter, too, some handsome trees and shrubs. Again, hardly any dwellings except a spare sod hut, intended for rangers and cowboys. It has been raining ever since we left Grand Island at 2.30 A. M. The inhabitants say Providence is sending rain as the boundaries of civilization advance; and aver they have hopes they shall lose no great time irrigating, after a number of years, as the rainfall will then suffice.

Breakfast we get late at North Platte, two hundred and ninety-one miles from Omaha, and two thousand seven hundred and eighty-nine feet already above sea level, with two thousand inhabitants; and some ten thousand cattle and sheep in sight. 10 A. M., we arrive at the village of Alkali, so called, an old ranger told me, on account of the much impregnated nature of the soil, whose surface water, thirty years ago, killed numerous animals and a few men who drank it. Artesian wells are already in requisition.

Ogallala signs: "General Store" — "Clothing at Cost" — "Saloon" — "O. K. Saloon" — "Post Office and Bakery" — "Rest for the Cow-Boys."

The Platte here is a shallow pond of scattered sand islands. On the flats feed three hundred or four hundred horses and ponies; twelve hundred or fifteen hundred cattle on the opposite side. Again, thousands; then forty or fifty. Cattle are shipped from along here for $5 per head to Chicago (twenty to a car) and average $40.

Sydney: four thousand and six feet high—good dinner of fish and vegetables. This country is somewhat bluffy, and scattered table rocks abound. Hills are becoming more decided; on them a few spruces are appearing. Some houses of railroad ties dot the bare plains, built much like our old Kentucky stockades, only with sod roofs. Cattle pens, or corrals, are made of the same, and old ties are used also for firewood. Those thrown along the track seem to have rotted easily—from the alkali, I suppose, as it would hardly be natural for native pine, spruce or hemlock to decay so rapidly of itself. Fifty-two miles from Cheyenne.

Pine Bluffs, from natural features so called, are a semi-circular range of rocky, wooded hills, rounding off beautifully to the left. The trees are, or look to be, stunted. To the right, the plain sweeps past a jut of headland. A storm mutters over it sullenly. Grass has been growing shorter, soil sandier. We pass a hut of logs with shingle front and a log and dirt stable. Signs: "I's Place" — "Saloon" — "Halo ther" — "Dry Goods and Groceries." Here are stable and plank stockades of slabs—also used extensively for out-houses in the mountains. Here we meet bluffs of crumbling rocks, pools of rain-water at their feet. The six hundred-mile plain stretches on ever the same.

Fifteen miles from Cheyenne. Tho' the grass is very thin and suitable for sheep-grazing, we see attempts to cut and cock it for hay. The hill ranges for scores of miles have been soft and undulating, with exceptions above. A few rocks and gravel are the sole next feature.

CHEYENNE, CAPITAL OF WYOMING,

sprang up the "Magic City of the Plains" in '67 with the advent of the Union Pacific Railroad. Catholics set up in '68, with a $9,000 church, of which Rev. T. J. Nugent is the present pastor. The city is just midway between Ogden and Omaha, five hundred and fifteen miles from each. Water is obtained from lake "Mahpalutah," three-quarters by three-eighths of a mile in extent. But ten or twelve inches of rain fall here during the year, I was informed by the Government meteorologist, a courteous Catholic gentleman. But few trees diversify the streets or yards and they decay soon. Grass and greenery are precious and cherished as jewels. The

plains in the neighborhood are illimitable, except towards the Rockies, and are thus very favorable for
building. They produce little more than sparse
blades of grass and a few weeds, and are very gravelly. Scattered wild blossoms sweeten the wild.
The spurs of the southern Black Hills rear in the
Northwest; and Long's Peak, one of the highest in
the main range, looms up grandly at a distance of
seventy-five miles. The range shows clefts in the
sunshine thirty miles away, and appears but twenty-
eight or thirty yards against the sky. This town of
five thousand inhabitants is already six thousand and
forty-two feet above sea level; the air is cool and
bracing in the dog days—even cold, now in August.
The country is blessed with sunshine nearly the year
round, even in dead of winter. As little rain, so
little snow, falls here; but the winds are described
as awful, when they sweep unobstructed down the
even plain, hedged by the mountains on but one
side.

August 4th, 11 *A. M.*—I start to Denver. At
Carr the hills are rolling; ruins, as of ground foundations, dot the hollows, and the prospect of the roll
and tumble of the hills to the Rockies reminds me
of the storm-heaving sea. The midchain on the
back-ground walls up the horizon by its huge bulk
peaked with summits of snow; and like the magnificent dome of Nature's temple, Long's Peak towers
majestic over all.

Eaton, Greeley, Evans—we leap suddenly from
a sandy, volcanicly sterile region into cultivated
farming oases, colored with great fields of fair
wheat, half-sized potatoes and corn. Harvest of

barley is **going on**. Evans is a bloom in **the desert**; **fine trees** towering up over the pretty prairie blossoms of yellow and purple, red and white ; corn fields, drilled and sown broadcast, wave green; and all this is **created** by artificial irrigation from the river (the South Platte), which flows crooked and well-wooded along the base of the foot hills on to Denver. If, on gazing at the bald-headed, snow-peaked Rockies, one exclaims in praise to **the Cre-ator**: "Thou, indeed, art Almighty God;" as he turns **to** the feats of little man in these newly-populated regions—vegetation produced from gravel **and sand** dunes and ant hills—cactus, **like great** green prickly human tongues, and sage not **half concealing the** arid ground—he **is** forced to add : "**Oh, powerful** man! thine image and likeness **is indeed of the Cre-ator**, and His work shines brightest **in thee, head of** Nature." Here's another plain mountain **townlet.** Canvas-roof house, **then a brick**; a saloon with great **canvas sign, "Railroad Crossing;"** a tent; "Saloon **and lunch room;" good** brick and sizable frame— and you have the photograph, instantaneous and perfect.

To Central City.

A storm of mist and rain just past as we push into the mouth of the mountains, now spanned by a glorious rainbow. The spurs rise, mottled, pillar-headed, on either hand. All the torrent-watered valley smiles with greenery of wild shrubs of cotton-wood, alder and willow. Little two-foot corn, whitish hay and greenish **oats**, some cut, dotted **along.**

Golden, a city shining with green vegetation, has fine buildings, in a rocking vale up and down the sides of the hemlock-flanked spurs. This is a tough climb for the grimy and griming little narrow-gauge up Clear Creek Canon, forty miles to Central in four hours—some hundred feet rise to a mile in distance. Queer series of towns or scattered houses, rather; mines; abandoned prospect holes and "dumps" fly slowly past, up and down the enormous gulches. All nationalities are working side by side, and all mixed—Chinese, Irish, Cornish, Welsh and Scotch; ' English and Yankees bossing the capital, Irishmen principally the labor.

ITEMS RELIGIOUS AND PROFANE ON THE ROCKIES.

In '59, the American Desert stretched from almost the Missouri River to the Rockies. Flour was sold at the very nominal value of $50 a sack. It may interest to jot some items of the older history of these parts.

In the cliff houses of Rio Mancos there lived the supposed descendants of the Aztecs. Later the Mexicans ascended as far as Pueblo. Indians inhabited

COLORADO.

As late as 1806 Colorado was a part of the French Louisiana Purchase. Jim Pursley, of Bardstown, Ky., was the first explorer before Pike, Long, James; or before even Fremont came in '43. Of the early history of Pueblo, Wilbur Stone says: "Game was plenty in early days and settlers frequently indulged in it during winter, both for food and pastime. It consisted chiefly of deer, antelopes, jack rabbits, monte and seven-up!" From '60 to '79, fifteen daily and fifty weekly papers have sprung up. The three thousand Ute Indians in Western Colorado have twelve million acres reserved for their use.

The average of the timber line is eleven thousand eight hundred feet; average height of mountains being eleven thousand feet. An average of seventy-two cloudy days in the year is calculated from the signal service since '63. Average snow, forty days.

From a pamphlet of '74, we learn of two hundred and fifty authenticated cures of asthma in this mountain country. Rheumatism and purely nervous diseases become worse, and mountain pneumonia prevails.

The geologists have it that in the tertiary period at Denver and Golden, there was a large swamp for hundreds of miles north into British Columbia and south into New Mexico, wherein flourished a luxurious vegetation, whose decomposition has resulted in the largest strata of tertiary coal in the valley of the Missouri.

In the Spanish part of the State there were churches at La Trinidad, La Costilla and Los Coneyos, with some dependent chapels.

As to Idaho. ·

the Jesuits from St. Louis received three delegations of Indians from '30 to '39, all begging for a priest. The Jesuits baptized six hundred of the Iroquois and Flatheads in six months. The first mission was founded in '41, and the Vicariate Apostolic included Idaho and Montana in '68. Population of Catholics in '78, 5,850—3,000 whites.

CATHOLIC PUEBLOS AND MISSIONS.

Not only can we claim that the Catholic Norsemen from Iceland founded churches in Greenland and Martha's Vineyard, just five hundred years before Plymouth Rock, and remained until an ice revolution from 60 degrees north destroyed the whole face of the country, but Dr. G. Shea proves that long prior to the Puritans there were three missions of religious: 1. Spanish Dominicans, Franciscans and Jesuits in the South, from Florida to California. 2. French Recollects and Jesuits from the St. Lawrence to the Pacific, and from the Gulf to Hudson's Bay. 3. English Jesuits in Maryland, of whom all but the last preceded the advent of any sect or minister.

The earliest friar, Mark of Nice, came in 1539, but had to relinquish the field of California and New Mexico in 1542. The expedition of Coronado reached the head-waters of the Arkansas, but turned back to the Rio Grande in the diocese of Santa Fe—Father Padilla and Brother John of the Cross only remaining and obtaining martyrdom at Quivira, just fifty years after Columbus and forty years after the Franciscans had poured out their blood in New Mexico. Others succeeded them and "all the tribes on the Rio Grande," whose towns are still extant, "were converted." In the next century, the Apaches destroyed many villages. New Mexico was conquered by the United States in '45 and annexed.

In 1768 Upper California was bereft of its Jesuit missionaries, who were immediately succeeded by the Franciscans and a few seculars. There were twenty-two missions there up to 1822. San Diego, Monterey and San Francisco had seventy-five thousand converts in 1825.

Mexico became free, and the Spanish missionaries being driven out, religion languished here and in Texas, which was French in the seventeenth century. There were martyrs in San Antonio and San Francisco. Religion has revived since the establishment of the Vicariate Apostolic in 1842.

The Catholic population of New Mexico is the largest, in proportion, of any State or Territory of the Union. The Catholic population **west of** the Mississippi River in 1882 **was** 1,461,500; the whole population in 1880, **11,282,000;** the Catholic population **being to the** whole as one to seven, about.

To Georgetown.

August 9th.—Wheat is being harvested, preceding a week or so, the cutting of hay, oats and barley; which latter, in the mountain valleys, is generally cut green, **in the** "milk," **to** serve as food for animals. Corn is thin and low, like the wheat, which is principally of spring variety, tho' I know of a field of oats seeding itself from the past **season.** Wheat **has** to **suffer** if not rained on **before it comes up, as** irrigation only **serves for later stages of growth.** Everything is green—vegetables **fresh, young lettuce,** peas, radishes, **etc.**

The cars make but ten miles an hour up the Canon, and ease down about at the same speed. As the proverb says, "Every blanket, its flea;" so every up-train its motes for the eye, by reason of its hard puffing.

Here we come to "pie-station," so called from the substantiality of refreshments in the shape of milk, coffee, sandwiches and pies, to satisfy the increased appetites sharpened by the rarifying air.

Cool, cooler as we branch off to the Georgetown Canon, and along the plunging, dashing Clear Creek, which comes nearer being a reality, by the cold, glassy waters foaming into pearlier beads and runs. Up this branch there is little gulch mining and no defilement of the torrents—the opening being much broader and finer than up to Central, as the gorge widens on either hand into grander slopes of now jagged and bony, now smoother and grassy flanks. Nor do we meet such precipitous overhanging masses. "Hills peep over hills"—profiles past profiles, where we see cows browsing the sweet grass on leveler ledges. Here is a level tract with angles of hills at 45 degrees; then great groves of pine trees, regular and beautiful—their paler spring or summer foliage comparing with their older needles, as pea with sea-green.

These hills—hills? They are as high as the average Alps — rise upwards of 2,500 and 3,000 feet above the torrent. This Georgetown and Central City measure respectively 8,400 and 8,510 feet, and you can ascend to over 14,000 feet above sea level in twelve miles of here, at Grey's or James' Peaks. So that instead of comparing these with the Alps, the Europeans must compare theirs with ours and say the "European Rockies" instead of our saying the "American Alps." The Alps ? The Alps average but 10,000 feet.

Coleridge's poem on Mt. Blanc and the Vale of Chamouni has double application in Colorado:

"Thou . . . most awful form . . .
 Risest from forth thy silent sea of pines
 How silently. . . . Sole sovran of the vale,
 Who sank thy sunless pillars in the earth?
 Who filled thy countenance with rosy light?
 Who made thee parent of perpetual streams?
 And you, ye five wild torrents fiercely glad!
 Who called ye forth from night and utter death,
 Down these precipitous, black, jagged rocks,
 Forever shattered and the same forever!
 Ye pine groves, with your soft and soul-like sounds!"

And Chas. Mackay poetizes on such "Mountain Tops:"

"The earth beneath them seemed as it had boiled,
 And tossed and heaved in some great agony;
 Like suddenly at fiat of the Lord
 The foaming waves had hardened into hills
 And mountains, multitudinous and high,
 Of jagged outline, piled and overpiled
 One o'er the other. Calmly the grey heads
 Of these earth-fathers pointed up to heaven;
 Titanic sentinels, who all the night
 Look at their kindred sentinels, the stars,
 To hear the march and tramp of distant worlds.
 Ye hills, I love ye! Oh! ye mountain tops,
 Lifting serenely your transcendent brows
 To catch the earliest glimpses of the dawn!
 It is a pain to know ye and to feel
 That nothing can express the deep delight
 With which your beauty and magnificence
 Fill to o'erflowing the ecstatic mind!"

Vegetation, in a chosen spot, is glorious for this altitude—gardens showing, farms broadening, among the gulches. We can not see the creek for the gross undergrowth, interlocked pines and spruces. Here are rich **patches** of grass and some healthy-looking potatoes. It is claimed the mountaineers can raise as fine potatoes as are wanted.

The strata of rock travel up to Idaho Springs **from below and down** from above, **this** point being their meeting place. And how beautifully shine with mica and metallic lustre some of these superb mountain flanks! Aladdin's cave turned inside out!

Friday—We arrive at Georgetown, of some 4,000 inhabitants, in an arm of the mountains—a flat **sand-level**, watered by the great roaring Clear Creek, **with** its tributaries from the Silver Plume gulches. The city is headed off by a mountain front, and walled **on either part by precipitous** half rock, half earth, altitudes of 2,200 feet to 3,000 feet above the town. **The ascent up one** side, to what is called Highland **Park, is so** great a climb, that it takes two hours **and one**-half of moderate travel on **foot to** make it; and **we, who have** been there, **can** aver that a man only finds **out, when too** late, what a fool he was **to go** up at all, as the ascent is of the hardest and least interesting, **and you** have but a poor prospect **when** you have reached the top. Some snow ranges; **the** little conic, white-streaked "Professor" looming **up** in a point: **Grey's** peak, looking lower, tho' higher: **the plains off towards** Denver appearing up over **the tops of the peaks;** the silvery line of the motionless **looking** torrents down the gulches, **and you have it** all in a sentence. Then comes a plunge down of an hour and one-half, breaking up the muscles **spared** in the ascent! And an act of contrition with a firm purpose of never doing so any more—and you have only to groan and ache the rest of the day over your **folly.**

August 10*th.*—We visit to-day with Fr. N. Matz, the pastor of the mountain city, the famous Green Lake, which report wants to place at 10,000 feet and which it scarcely reaches; as Highland makes only 10,400 by the instrument, and the lake is near seven hundred feet below this. The extent of the really bottle-green and glass-clear lakelet, embedded between a rough hewn tumble of rocks dressed in shaggy pines, and a shady, graveled shore, is three-quarters of a mile long, by about three-eighths of a mile wide. The bottom, visible for twenty-five or thirty feet, is a rough, rocky funnel, some seventy-five feet at the deepest, while the walls ascend 1,500 to 2,200 or 2,300 feet above. You mount to the Lake by a zigzag route up the Clear Creek bed until you reach a fine forest of almost untouched growth. We had a row on the placid green bosom, reflecting the mountains and pines, and visited the "Battle of the Gods," an awful tumble of granite bowlders and stones, heaped up like a pyramid in ruins and copped by a wigwam-like, open cave, called "Cave of the Winds;" whence you descend by leaps to the lake edge. This is the poetic fruit of the visit:

GREEN LAKE OF THE ROCKIES.

Chaste emerald lake!
Snow nursling, awake!
Thou crystal, pure fountain,
In lap of the mountain,
Art child of the steep and the sky.
Snow Naiads,
Star Pleiads—

God's angels erst courted thine eye.
Ere earth-wrack had torn thee
And time-fret had **worn** thee,
Thou mirror of light in **the** hills!
In spring rime
Of old time,
Thou fruitful wert mother of rills.
Yet, creamy white daughters
Of molten-glass waters
Make glad by their laughing,
As mountain wine quaffing,
Bead-foaming they bound to the river.
How calm thine increase,
In rock eyrie of peace,
Green well-spring of torrents forever!
Thy tossed rocks
And torn walls,
Thy pine locks
And foam falls
But make thy serenity grander.

———————

So pray we,
Oh! may we
Survive the first **ruins** of birth,
Reflect heaven's light upon earth;
And in the strong **hour**
Of self-possessed **power—**
In earth-seeming madness
Give waters of gladness,
To green o'er our sadness,
As to eternity's ocean we wander.

A school of fat trout are nurtured and fed by hand
near the shore; they are above ordinary size and are
fairly spoiling for a fry. Strangers are not allowed
to fish. There are two other basins, or hatcheries

for the smaller and smallest fish, in the shape of wood-walled and rock-bound tanks or reservoirs.

Little frail mica shales that you grind to powder in your fingers, with gneiss, quartz and mineral ore, form this mighty spinal column of the Western World. But all the mass seems—is, disintegrating and falling to ruins. They have frequent scurries of rain and snow in this spot. In the first days of August, last year, came a fall of snow, and twelve inches the 15th of July before, while fifteen inches covered Georgetown, August 29th, 1882. Snow falls almost every month in the year in some part of the mountains; still sunshine prevails six-sevenths of the year.

How bright and fresh the young city in the lap of the mountains! The light is the white light, bright light of the sunny East, whose Lebanons and Olympuses it reflects — whose ruggeder Sharons and Carmels. The rough-faced flanks glow with reflected sun-light ; and when we add the magic silver and gold heart of the mountains set in brilliant crystals and pyrites, one is fairly in dreamland. In sight of this we sing:

A SONG OF THE MOUNTAINS.*

Ye rock-pine ranks
　　And nascent rivers,
On mountain flanks—
　　O lesson-givers!
I would ye fire
　Earth's ruined eclipse,
And sky-inspire
　These earth-sealed lips!

*Published in the "Ave Maria," September, 1883.

  For sin-mad few
   Have marred what God hath done;
  And nothing new
   Is now beneath the sun.
How looketh all unto a primal state,
And Nature, like its unthroned monarch, Man,
Stands ghastly, oft, a ruin of itself.
So stood the ruined Archangel at his fall.
—Were these sheer peaks not lordlier erst?
       Nor shot
Them down below yon earth-heaped vale?
      And what
Hath scalped these summits of their verdant locks,
And left them open to the tempest's rage—
Their foreheads ploughed, like Satan's, lightning-scathed?
Were they but unclean vessels then as now,
To hold the broken corpses of the steeps—
By Death-sin felled, and hurled by rodent Time!
The plain—saith Nature's seer—quiescent earth,—
While mountain labors and dismembers self,
As quakes its aspen, and its stately pine
Hangs rigid arms and wrings pale hands in woe;
Anon, the tear-stains soil the sensive rocks,
Whose tear-drops steal adown their rugged cheeks,
To swell the floods of wounded Nature.
      Thus,
Its lord, created on a pinnacle,
So little less than angels that they sought
His converse, and sweet symphonied about
The jasper walls of Eden.   Man looked,—
Creation crouched submissive at his feet
To learn its name.   He, ruined hierarch,
Was stricken from his height, for pride and lust,—
Was shiftless goaded down the steep, to fight
His Mother Earth for suck, and ward his life
From rebel brutes, revenging God 'gainst man.

The mountain torrents nearest native snows,
Unsullied, sparkling, leap and glad the heart—

Until they **touch** the **haunts of men.**   Then, fouled
By contact, haste the murky waters on,
Awaking mountain-echoes with their roar
Of pain at chastity defiled.

                     Pure winds,
The breath of mountain peak and vale—sisters,
Unsmirched as they, of glass-pure waters, sigh
Of unflecked stars and heaven, until they **soar**
About the smoking mines and hives of men.
Thus all, **befouled by** sinful creature, wreaks'
Revenge on him and his who ruined all.
—**No hope ?**
        Forbid it God, and Christ who died!

The millions of fingers
Of armies of singers
Point up from on high—
From their ranks in the sky!
        Their green arms not swinging,
        Nor silvered hands wringing,
        But strong arms outflinging,
        To lift to the height.
Their red crests aglow
'Gainst driftings of snow,
They hail after sunset
—Yet gilding the runlet—
        The kindling of camp-fires,
        Ignited from cloudland;
      —'Tis trysting of war
        Of the Pines and the Star!
        In sammets and sapphires,
        A king o'er his proud band,
        The Prince doth appear,
        With his glittering spear—
        Bright harbinger, Eve-star,
        Leads on to the sky war.
To clamber the blue height,
And conquer the Old Night—
Unbending and proud,

Their banner the cloud,
The phalanx of Pines
Storm up the inclines!

Such, Christian, the lists
Of the armies of Christ:
So, e'en thro' the mists
Of the twilight of wrath,
Must *ye* seek the path
To the mountain of tryst.
  By gluttony, pride,
  By duties denied,
  Ye fell from the right!—
  March on up the height,
  Like your brothers, the Pines,
  Unbending to winds
  And hurtling storms.
Not angelic forms,
But *mankind* have trod
These mountains of God.
  E'er Christ-led
  And Christ-fed:
  All tearless
  And fearless,
  Storm sky-height
  By Christ-light,
  And, wavering never,
  Wear laurels forever!

These heights are growing on me. What I took
to be 500 or 700 feet high has shot up to three or
four times as much and not exceeded the reality.
The bold headlands about here are many above
timber line, some probably 12,000 feet high, and upwards of 3,500 or 4,000 above town. Green Lake is
1,500, and thence we can see mountain heads above

us certainly 2,000 or more feet higher. It took
Stanley and the astronomers of the total eclipse a
couple of years ago, some three or four hours to
reach such a spot from this Green Lake. There is a
flag staff on top of the highest, left there by the
party of scientific climbers.

To Silver Plume.

August 11th.—Up the gorge or open Canon, to
the right of Georgetown. The new railroad, whose
track is just being laid and bridges built, takes this
wind, always rising about 200 feet per mile, in perfect lines of curve, with five bridges, one seventy-
five feet high: the line of road runs along the base
of the great masses on the left and in front of Georgetown; crosses the creek-torrent; doubles back on
itself over the high bridge, then ascends; crosses
twice again, once more redoubles and finally takes a
long sweep up. Silver Plume is 500 feet higher
than Georgetown, situated in a little lap of the gorge,
the sublime rocks, towering to thousands of feet on
both sides of the silver-foam torrent, rushing past
and around the houses, some of which are built in
fancy styles. Off to the left rears the bald Elephant
Back, 12,000 feet; to the right swings the mighty
hill, and the great jutting rock-land rises beyond, a
background imposing and beautified by a fringe of
fine spruces, one of which, specially remarkable for
its height and symmetry, forms the apex to a solitary peak of piled granite.

Middle Park, Colorado.

Sunday, Aug. 12th.—To Middle Park, on Frazier
River, over Empire Pass, which our æronoid regis-

ters at 8,500, to Empire, 8,400 feet. As we rise on
the flank of the rocks the valley widens and deepens
to the vision; the little town in Clear Creek Canon
some couple of miles below, with its superb grove of
native pines, puts on a picturesque air, and the
mountain walls rise and roll in their majesty, forming
the ascent to the high distant sky. Glorious! Winding down over the creek at the bottom of Empire-
town, we circle to the left and toil along a fine
gravel road up the Canon and past the beautiful
pine and harvest-green valley of Empire. This is
capable of being an extended town, stretching back
and forth thro' the higher sides of the inclining flat
to the creek. Passing further, we come to a fine
race-track on a good level and surrounded by pine
groves and willow brush. Great dalles of rock close
in the torrent; and as the pass narrows, the mountains swing off more sublimely to the right and left,
until we come to the grandest pile I saw in the.
foot-hills of the Rockies, the famous "Skull Promontory," so-called because of its peculiar representation of a human head-piece. In a general pro-
file it resembles, however, a gigantic stair-case, of
more or less regular steps, such as one might imagine
to be the lower flight of that Godly way down
which He, who has His tabernacle in the sun, descends with mighty leaps to earth. "He comes,
skipping over the hills."

ODDITIES AMONG SUBLIMITIES.

Ah! here's the "Atlantic House"—a fine good-
lettered gold sign, on a black sanded ground, attached

to a house—well! a big box three-fourths of a story,
opposite a saw-dust pile.   On one end a hotel:
ahem! on the other, a bar room with a pair of deer-
horns over the entrance.   A little farther on and we
come to a new "camp," where extensive mills and
boarding house are nearly completed and a town
commenced of one-half dozen or so shanties of log
and boards; all springing, they say, out of an inspiration of some fool spiritualist, with spare cash of his
own (or may be somebody else's).   He knew by
mediums there was a fine prospect for a good mine
in these rugged hills.   So far it has panned out nothing—but a hole in the hills.   Passing the toll-gate,
where we pay nearly $6 toll, we strike the foot of the
range on a superb mountain road, level and well kept.
And we are delighted to greet an abundance of wild
flowers: American blue-bells, heliotropes, mountain
daisies — very aster-like — and little dew-drop lilies,
roses *en masse*, and at all stages from tiny buds, to
full-blown, deep-blushing, full dress.

At 5.20 P. M., we reach 10,000 feet and see skipping about the old robin and the new magpie, the
latter looking pretty rusty and bachelor-like in his
neglige and ruffled plumage of black and white.
Smaller chippers dot the fir boughs.   Looking down
thro' a rift in the dense forest, we see the clouds drifting in the gorges, and by the mountain sides and
tops; while the torrent calls from 2,000 feet below,
and the mingled scent of pine gum and snow rein-
vigorates the uptoilers.   In front is a great sharp
backbone of the Red Elephant, the naked sides like
fine keel.   At 10,250 flowers follow scantier; and
climbing 200 feet of a short cut of sixty degrees in-

clination, we fall upon the reddest, red roses and buds sweet as can be imagined in their first blush in the hard world and against the rugged, time-stained rock faces. Whitened stems of the pines on the opposite mountain show Nature frozen out in the attempt to scale the sides, while we, ourselves, begin to tuck our clothes about us more closely, and add to them to keep out the ever more chilling air. Here we discover our first Indian pinks, a kind of Indian, fusky red, of rather coarse texture, pretty, a way off.

BERTHOUD PASS.

At the top of the Pass, at 6.20 P. M., we halt to lunch and breathe. We are on the continental Divide; and from a swing, tied in the bough of a fir, we can enjoy the sensation of one minute breathing the air of the Atlantic, the next of the Pacific slope. James' Peak, off to the right with its snow-patched head, seems only a rifle shot or two away, tho' it remains that far and more for over an hour of travel towards it. We knock at the perfectly cruciform log inn at the top for a drink of coffee, but "the water has not boiled," and we drink California sherry. We are glad to get down out of the chilling cold— tho' the grass is emerald green beside the snow patches and potatoes flourish below—into the more genial latitude of 9,400 feet.

The triple source of the Frazer leaps down across our path in brilliant amber waves and beady foam. Green meadows of great, long grasses glide swiftly past us; while, opposite in the setting sun-rays, the solid mounts of pine sweep up alongside the burnished king's becker of California gold, redly glow-ing, and **stretching above in the** mountain heights **to** within a **few** degrees of zenith. Having taken **four** hours to labor up the **A**tlantic slope, we scud down **the** Pacific, twelve miles, in just 1.35 by the watch.

Monday morning we had two Holy Masses at

Cozen's Ranche,

a good roomy and porched frame, capable of **com**fortably accommodating twenty-odd besides the family, and on a pinch some thirty-seven or thirtyeight, as has been practically proven. This is situated below Vasquez's Creek, a branch of the Frazer, which again feeds the Grand River, and is the inevitable and much-sought resort of travelers from the "outside" and the "inside," as the mountaineers call the ultramontane and cismontane regions. The entertainment is of the best—the fat of the land and of the water—in the shape of all the diverse wild game and mountain trout. Superadded fruits and even moun**tain** vegetables help **to** regale the sore and hungry traveler, who blesses the soldierly host and his kind deft lady and daughters for their fine inn and all it represents; praising it **as** the very best place **for a** stoppage anywhere about Middle Park.

Cowboys and Gentler Folk.

One meets every variety of traveler here, like in the famed old English and Scotch taverns—from the devil-may-care, **but** really often kind-hearted **cowboy, to the** polished gent from the **East, who between** fishings, dons his **fine** garters and **knee-breeches, puts** on a fresh "biled shirt" **and** sports a **necktie.** 'Tis true, the cow-boy—who **is not,** however, **either cow** or boy, but a fullgrown steer on his hind legs—does

not generally indulge in the expense of lodging under
a roof more pretentious than a log-and-mud hut or
rough-hewn ranche hostelry. He is of the genus
vagabond on horseback, and as often as not ties his
horse to a stake, flings the saddle and blanket on the
bosom of mother earth, tucks his own robe and yellow rain-proof about him and snores away under the
canopy of heaven—ready to snort himself awake
when his turn for guard over the herd is whooped
into his ear by his indelicate comrades. But if he be
off duty and has received his $30 monthly wages, and
finds an opening for a social drink, drunk and "round-
up," he is as free with his cash as his oaths and
"damns" if "he isn't ready to *holler*"—as he expresses
his desire to turn into his gentle couch, when the
shades of night have fallen and the mists of his "rye"
mount to his brain. But gentler folk frequent the
park ranches—the refined family, with lady-wife and
smooth-cheeked little ones; the summering barrister
and bachelor merchant with their files of city papers
and copies of "Punch," "Ledger," and the like to
supply the room of their inevitable "Morning Journal" and "Evening Post;" the journeying students
with virgin rod and unfired gun—softly persuasible
by the "cock-and-bull" stories of the bear hunter,
deer-stalker and promiscuous mountain villain. In
the little tap-room—which happens to rejoice in no
tap, except that in the private pocket of each provi-
dent traveler—you see groups about the stove of the
various men-folk of the rougher sort, while the ladies
and cultured gentry resort to the lace-curtained and
tastily-uphostered parlor, not devoid of its cabinet
organ and many tinted chromos and family photos.

But the exquisites of all betake them to their private apartments, amusing themselves between selecting their "flies" for trout with literary small talk, puns and amorous discussions. Anon they turn them to their more serious occupation of the toilet, buff, buttoned pumps, sweet straw hats and snuff-colored knee-breeches — ah! pantaloons — trunk-hose! I will not soon forget the harsh expression of a rough pair of prospectors, with their horse and pack-ass trudging about for gold, whom we met and lunched with, when we described to them our fine gentlemen aforesaid. "Bah!" said they, with grim humor, "wouldn't we like to take them fellers out and stick 'em up to their neck in some of these sloughy bottoms—roll 'em over in the mud and spile their duds!" Such is the rougher Westerner's estimate of his Eastern fellow-man who comes out fishing with a Saratoga trunk·

In Frazer Creek Valley.

In this even valley of sage on one side and mostly good grass on the other, one is in a basin surrounded by three tiers of hills leading up to the James' on S. E., Long's on N. E., the snow range on three sides — the rocky peaks, especially on the east being jagged and angular. This mountain meadow is part of a system that extends for upwards of a hundred miles, they say, in all directions. Sheltered and cool is it all, with generally rich, though not always sightly grass. Cattle fatten wondrously here. And haying is as fine as in the Black Forests of Baden or the Valleys of Switzerland, yielding the firmest, richest butter and cream, thick as good molasses.

There was, just as we entered, a goodly herd of

one **hundred** and forty-four head, summering since **June and** tho' bought, thin and poor all the way from Iowa, for some eighteen dollars per head, for two **and** three years old, ten to twelve dollars **for** yearlings, and twenty calves, they sold for $4,500, the sellers losing on account of great cost of carriage.

Our tent pitched, ditched and swung, instead of poled, we set out fishing and hunting. The hunting now, as afterwards, yielded us little small game, the birds consisting of chicken and bird-hawks, a good many robins and a few scattered twitterers. But our fishing yielded us sixteen or seventeen sweet trout, two or three fingers broad, long as your hand, or hand and wrist, from the by-flowing Frazer at our side. This was brook and spring for all purposes. A few slices of our streaked fat-and-lean bacon, good rye loaves, a brimming pot of strong but groundy **coffee, milk** and sugar to taste, with our already **acquired** mountain appetite, made a meal right more than royally enjoyed by the six of us down-squatters and etiquette-forgetters. After a very amateur pistol practice, in which we studiously avoided the bull's-eye and sometimes missed the good-sized trunk of a pine, we fished again; a new hand or two catching their first trout. What beauties with golden and silvery silk skin of the varied hues, from lightest to near the darkest browns and greens, delicate as butterflies, fine **as** colored meerschaum !

First Night Out.

This bright day goes down in a painting sun and orange clouds. The camp-fire is smoking for supper **and** sixteen trout with some accompaniments are

served. War-whoop call and pan-beating are scarcely
needed to keen youth. Fine night before us, three-
quarter moon half up the sky and our spirits mount-
ing with it. God's angels guard my first night out!

> "Huc, custos, igitur pervigil advola,
>   Avertens patria de tibi credita
>   Tam morbos animi quam requiescere
>   Quidquid non sinit incolas."

Which stanza of the Church's Guardian Angel
hymn may be rendered:

> "Then hither, fly succoring, Guardian sleepless,
>   Averting from fatherland trusted to thee,
>   Distorted diseases of fancy—whatever
>   Makes Sleep its inhabitants flee!"

August 14*th.*—Ugh! awfully cold night. Ice on
our bucket and heavy frost coming in our open tent
slit. I got chilled so thoroughly in the shoulders and
back lungs that I crouched up to my companions
and kept them awake. Whisky and rubbing lasted
for only an hour or two—the hills, not to say mountains of cold, pressed down upon me and made me
fear a risk of pneumonia. It reminds me forcibly of
that other miserable night of nights in my youth,
when three or four of us boys were taken up by the
negro soldiers about this day and date in 1862, and
marched off to their camp in the suburbs of Louisville, Kentucky—so kept all night in our summer
jackets, without tent or sufficient fire and made to
work on the fortifications against Morgan the next
morning. My God, it hurt!

Ho! ho! you may imagine some one was glad to
see morning and two of us were out fishing by 5 A.
M., scarcely light. We thrashed the Frazer lustily

for upwards of two hours, and got nothing for our pains but an enormous load of appetite for our meagre breakfast on some fried potatoes and three fried fish! We eked out with our staple rye bread, rough butter, and groundy coffee. All soon disappeared. We did better for dinner—had, between us, ten fair troutkins. It seems from repeated experiments that trout will not bite early in the morning, the very time for most other fish. At any other times, say from nine or ten o'clock to eleven or twelve at night, they take hold readily, if one knows how to "fly" or bait them. We regaled on five or six for supper. To-day I killed some game; a fine jack-rabbit of six or eight pounds weight, small birds and a squirrel, two-thirds the size of our southern grey, with foxy tail, white belly, and dark grey back, blackish snout and paws. I spent this

OFF EVENING AT THE CAMP

conversing with our Captain. He is a Stonyhurst College man of eight years study, English ways and fine off-hand manners, generous as his Irish nature, enterprising manager of the "Pay Rock" mines and mills, running over one hundred hands and paying him $350 a month. Mr. J. M. S. Egan, tho' evidently well informed, is modest withal, and it was only by dexterous questioning I got out something of his history and college life. He has a brother a Benedictine, and a sister, a nun, I think. One of his old college chums is editing the Stonyhurst College Journal, and Mr. Egan is collecting a cabinet of mineral ores for him and his old Alma Mater. It seems the Alumni have a regular club-room in Dublin with

officers to conduct it in the style of a good private
hotel, furnished with library, billiards, etc. Here the
old graduates meet from all parts of the world and
representing all professions. Their standard and
grade are very high here as well as at Downside—the
Benedictines and others, as evidenced by their pupils
taking many first prizes in the University contests·

My other two companions, the cousins Guanella,
Italian by name but thorough Americans and fairly
educated, are fine young fellows. They made it very
pleasant for all by their hearty enjoyment of our daily
sport and mutual reports of feats and disasters.

The Assumption in Middle Park.

August 15th.—Ah ! Our Lady's—bless her forever! We had the consolation of Holy Mass at
Cozen's Ranche in their cozy parlor, and the whole
family went to their duties, glad to get the chance of
seeing a priest two or three times a year. Our men
assisted, of course, and the Captain served Mass in
good remembrance of his school days. We enjoyed
an excellent meal with the family and went home to
camp for a big hunt and a big "fish." We—the
Guanellas and I—went eight or ten miles up into one
of the mountain gorges, winding around with our
team, thro' the patches of grass, and ascended some
seven hundred or eight hundred feet higher to *hunt*
elk. We saw some tracks more or less mouldy, had
a hard old tramp and climb over dismal broken
ground and fallen timber in the hot sun for hours,
and brought back a rabbit, squirrel and plover,
bless the mark! Our friend Egan, who went fishing, had got never so much as a bite, and we settled

ourselves down to a capital, but rather greasy, rabbit-stew, which he had the fortune to condiment with corn, vegetables and oranges, obtained from a traveling huckster. Our next neighbors moved their camp to-day and we are alone.

This whole valley and the next on the right have been lake-beds, seven or eight miles long by two and one-half or three broad. The banks rise visibly on all sides and are bluffy in one point, several small streams feeding the Frazer from Crooked and Ranche Creeks. The right valley, watered by the latter creek, seen from a precipitous promontory is beautiful at a distance with its straggling riverlet and great soft bunches of green willow.—Musquitoes are so thick they won't let me write any more to-night.

August 16*th*.—I could not say Mass on account of an old gentleman prostrated with nervous debility occupying the parlor at Cozen's.

The sunset was fine yesterday. The floating clouds flaunted their waving red-tinted banners about the heads of the mountains "like flaming locks of hair," to use Ruskin's comparison. As the sun disappeared the long rays gilded the green foot-hills and threw deepening shadows aslant and atop. The rocky caps over timber line, refining more and more in the red rays, changed their dull gold to brighter sheen and tints pinker and deeper—so threw the snow drifts into whiter prominence, like rising foam in burnished beckers. We found strawberries, small but spicy in flavor, in the spurs and picked away as we waited for the deer to come. They didn't arrive.

I got up at six and finding the boys asleep at camp, the early bird had to wait—for its worm! We had better luck fishing—bagged two dozen, counting three we hooked out in the dark and couldn't recover. Boys tell magniloquent marine stories about their fishing, but we count *heads*.

A Cowboy Story.

Our Stonyhurster has had great sport "codding" a neighboring cowboy of genuine greenness and profanity, telling him of the feats of the priest. The said cowboy, a youth of some twenty-one years, shock-hair, belt and big spurs, thought the priest rather quiet. "But then you had to look out for them quiet fellers—by gosh!" He smothered his curses in my presence, but couldn't restrain himself in Egan's vicinity and would damn for everything and nothing. Egan made him believe that the priest could, with a pistol in each hand, knock bottles at thirty paces right and left, hitting his mark every crack. And he cursed and damned if that wasn't "powerful shootin'." The priest could hang on the side of a horse and lasso out of a herd any cow or steer he pleased by *both* horns: "Ge—menentely! I've been at the business twelve years, and d—n my skin if I could ever hook but *one* horn!" Egan played the game well for he knew the fellow had to leave early next morning with his herd. But the cowboy swore: "If I didn't fear bein' docked, I'd come over and see that priest shoot and ride."

The mountains look grander with storm clouds for a back-ground than in sunshine. Their bold

summits loom up dark and distinct in shade from the
cloudland.   The green pines take a deeper, solemner
hue.   The thunder mutters and rolls longer and the
crashes are full of sublimity.   Where could one more
enjoy the thrill of awful pleasure felt in a rattling
storm than here!   Where more realized the glorious
hymn of the Psalmist King and poet: "The voice of
the Lord upon the waters; the God of Majesty hath
thundered, the Lord upon many waters.   The voice
of the Lord in power; the voice of the Lord in magnificence."   You hear "the voice of the Lord," as he
breaketh the cedars on the very mountains above
you.   "Yea, the Lord shall break the Cedars of Lebanon."   See as in the forked tongues "the voice
of the Lord divideth the flame of fire."   Imagine the
reality of "the voice of the Lord preparing the stags,"
on these very jungled heights; "and He will lay
open the thick woods" they inhabit.   And in this,
His most gloriously mountain walled "Temple," indeed, "all shall speak His glory." (Ps. 28.)

It rained to-night.

August 17th.—Raining yet—a good shower, accompanied by rumbling, reverberating thunder
We are not having good luck fishing, but somehow
always manage to scrape a meal together.   Sometimes we hear of two professionals, now staying at
Cozen's, from New York, catching upwards of a
hundred trout a day—we suppose it true, but never
counted them.   We heard of an elk cow and calves
at the head of Crooked and St. Louis Creeks, twelve
miles up.

What a consolation to get some letters in these
untaught wilds, especially when they have been for-

warded three **times**! Bless my soul's friends, they never desert me in all my wanderings.

To estimate the height of this valley, or park as they call all the lower levels and grass plots in these parts, **one** has only to look out and **see** the clouds skirting the pines on the rises of the foot-hills, some 9,000 feet high. Numerous cloud-banks weigh down between the higher steeps and the snow-patched range. We are nearly in storm-cloud region. At 5,280 feet to a mile, we are one and one-half mile high on this level; and can climb to over two miles and find men working mines, such as the "Ruby," owned and run by Barbee & Co. of Louisville, Kentucky, twelve miles from Grand Lake.

August 18th.—We ate breakfast this morning, literally, in the clouds. Chilly. Two of us went fishing on Ranche Creek and caught two dozen but **one**, after striking the wrong place for fish, wading and getting stuck in the mud, horse and foot, in the sloughy bottom, that looked so softly green and poetical from the bluff just anon. We came home wet and worn. Our mountains with "the hair floating from their fiery foreheads," reminded me of smoking volcanos ready to belch—or just having belched—flame and lava. It sweetens our pleasure toils to observe the features of the not beautiful but sublime section of these, the advance hills of the Rockies.

The Guanellas struck off afoot to hunt deer, and aver by everything truthful that they made forty-odd miles, which may be whittled down to twenty-five

and then be considered awful. All they got for
their tire and foot soreness was the glorious surplus
of exercise and a pint-cup nearly full of diminutive
strawberries. Bears, elk, deer, mountain-lions, saw
they none, and brought not even their tracks back.

A Deer-Capital Prize.

August 19*th.*—Oh! But people must not think us
so verdant as to come away from the Rockies deer-
less, bearless and all. To-day we secured the capital
prize—a glorious buck elk, some six or seven years
old, and kicking the beam at probably eight or nine
hundred pounds, gross weight. And the manner of
its drawing was this: We had some nearest neighbors—nearly as green as ourselves, by the way, and
in your ear—who, having pitched camp in our
grove, had gone out the previous evening to hunt
elk resorts, and stalk or wait for them near by.
Miller, an ear-whiskered New Yorker, and his com-
rade found a "lick"—something very like a hog-
wallow, and trampled with innumerable elk tracks—
in a spur of the hills, back of Crooked Creek Valley.
They were making ready to hide and squat for the
night, when fortunately up came the buck, within
fifty yards of them, unsuspecting and standing
quietly with his hindquarters exposed from behind
a tree. Miller took his chance and sent a great rifle
ball crashing thro' its buttocks, piercing thro' and
thro', and sprawling the poor beast, dragging its
helpless hind legs. As he crawled a few yards on
his front feet, the hunter came up with him, scram-
bling on some fallen pines, and shot him in the head,
keeling him over half upright on some horizontal

trunks. The two men fell on him, cut and hacked
at him with a jack-knife—more like a pocket-dag-
ger—until they sawed the body in two. After much
grunting and stumbling under the dead weight of
some three hundred and fifty pounds, they succeeded
in getting the hindquarters down the hill to the
mouth of a grassy park, and hung it by prising on
the lower limbs of a shaggy pine. Finding they
could do no more that night, they traveled to camp by
moonlight, arriving there in time to catch our Egan
on his way back from Cozen's at about 11.20 P. M.
Egan saw the verdancy of the chaps by the silvery
light; and knowing they had no team, put up a job
to haul over their game for *half* the carcass and *all*
the credit of killing. "Agreed"—it was just what
they wanted, minus, of course, the latter clause of
the contract, which our man prudently suppressed.
We got a start by nine o'clock after Holy Mass, and
by ten we pushed out of camp, with a "Hip, hip, hur-
rah! ho! for the mountains!" all armed cap-a-pie—
two rifles, two shot-guns, three revolvers, and two
butcher-knives! We had to make a great round of
some seven or eight miles, and then succeeded in
getting our team within but a mile or two of the
lick. It was 12 M., when we spied the grand hams
hanging from the pine and started up the hill with
bated breath and cocked guns towards the lick, talking of naught, in mysterious tones, but lions, bears,
etc., eating the carcass, and the probability of our
having to fight for the remains. It was exciting—
painfully so for greenhorns and "tender-feet"—the
latter being the name for everything fresh and un-
sophisticated in the mountains. The most danger-

ous thing that we encountered was the remains of
the deer, whole and intact and dead as a door nail.
The lick, however, was freshly trampled and showed
how ignorant the hunters were that they had not remained and got another shot or two. While the
butchers were getting the head off and the quarters
divided, I took a stroll out in the jungle of pines and
fine quaking aspens, as high as the spruces, with
smooth, light green trunks, bare to nearly the top.
I must confess to a feeling of shyness, not to say
anxiety, when I had got out of ear-shot of the party.
So after contemplating nature but a moment I returned—bearless. The head and horns being pre-
sented to me, I thought it proper I should "toat" it
down, which I did, swinging the head back of mine,
and holding by the reversed horns. I found afterwards I had bloodied my duster, pants and boots
from my neck to my heels. At the big pine we
packed the quarters on the horses, slung the head on
a pack-stick and processioned down the hill-park
to the wagon. We got back to camp after a nearly
eight hours' trip, dinnerless, tho' pleased and
"enthused." Oh! how we did eat elk for our din-
ner-supper!

After good night-fall one of our boys fished out
by moonlight the finest trout of the week, three in
number, one weighing just fourteen ounces. This
rounded our hundred trout caught for the whole trip.

I find peculiar calculations having to be made in
the mountains. They manufacture pumps with six
or seven feet difference of suction from what they
would be in the valley or plains. This peculiarity
regards weighing and dynamics also. There are no

lightning rods in the whole region, I understand; none being needed, tho' electrical displays are of daily occurrence. I don't recall a day in which I heard no thunder or saw no rain in some direction or other. Of these mountain parks, I heard the story contradicted by an old hunter, that lightning would play about fire arms in a storm at this height.

August 23*d*.—This the date of our camp break-up, when our Captain profaned the good old Irish emigrant ship-song by paraphrasing it, as applied to our wagon-ship:

> All at 10 o'cl'k in the morning oh!
> Our gallant ship set sail—
> With "Pickles," "Dan," two quarts of oats,
> And a pint of yellow *male!*

Which would require a good deal more of glossing to make its elegant appropriateness apparent to the poetical reader, than it would of choice and pruning of words to make it smoother and less truthful. "Pickles" and "Dan" were our steeds and knowing ones they were, as their names indicate, and the rest of the verse comprises in laconic conciseness the amount of provender left for man and beast after our ten days' camping. No particular adventure marked or marred our return, except the unfortunate circumstance that our elk-shooters had the meanness to tell how *they* had shot that animal *we all* shot and circumlocutorily lied around for most bravely. But then we stayed all adverse stomachs and allayed all unjust suspicions of our integrity in being able to let folk be deceived without direct impugning of the known truth, by simply letting the

ranche folks have a fore leg of our booty, in part
exchange for some dozens of fat trout we innocently
brought to Georgetown as the result, remotely, of
our dexterity in fishing, and otherwise, in the Park.
It's only a pity and great loss to the public our ex-
ploits had not been telegraphed like President
Arthur's.

Grand Lake, Colorado.

Grand Lake, Col., September 1st, 1883.

TO Grand Lake, in express and four-in-hand. We had an old-time stage driver who could swear on occasion, regardless of surroundings, and whip up according to approved customs of brutality to animals. We were nine—ten with the driver—but two went on ahead as outriders, one of them a joking lawyer whose aching tooth was jumping almost as much as his horse. Starting at 9 A. M., we arrived at Cozen's by about half-past three, and at Ostrander's by 6½ P. M., killing a grouse by the roadside and seeing no other small game but a squirrel or two feeding on the fine cones. Primitive place, the latter, situated in desolate gravel and sand beds, and surrounded, at a distance, by curiously water-fretted rocks and sage heaths, supplemented by the raggedest pine fellings. After a thorough search no game could be scared up in the whole vicinity; and on being further assured by an honest-spoken mountaineer of whom we inquired—"Be d—d, if he ever saw any grouse hereabouts"—we gave up the hunt. The hostler had hanging, around his characteristic waiting-room, some deer and doe hides and pretty spotted kid's furs as large as a small cur's skin. They ornamented the walls between the elk-horns and heads and the rifle racks above the doors. The body of the house is of logs—pines make first-class timber for such—and has batten doors only, on the outside and partly down stairs; the traditionary make-shift of blankets over the other door openings being supplied by cheaper cotton or calico hangings. The inside is gorgeously papered all over with every sort of imaginable odds and ends of New York story paper pictures, giving an elegant finish, and frescoing even the ceilings, *a la* Rockies. All the party but one slept soundly: there was no difficulty in hearing the snorers between the cracked partitions from any quarter.

Off by early and nasty breakfast—as the supper had been before it—we got on, thro' the winding valleys, to Grand Lake by dinner on Sunday. Better fare, if not quarters, awaited us, and we were ready for everything in the shape of tasty edibles.

Grand Lake.

This really not misnamed lake is two to two and one-quarter miles in length by about three-quarters of a mile wide—seems, however, very much larger to both gazer and rower. 8,700 to 8,800 feet above sea-level, it is walled in on all but the village and out-let sides by gloriously swelling spurs. Its head is fronted by the superb dome-like mass of Round Mountain. Pity it was not christened Grand Dome, for it needs but a Titanic proportioned cross to crown its summit in order to constitute it a more magnificent than Rome's Pantheon, raised aloft on St. Peter's colossal transept. The cyclopic *V* formed by the swinging heights on either side of Round

Mountain and framing it in—their snow-patched ridges rising shoulder and shoulder above even their mightier rocky dome—form a picture of grandeur satisfying the soul as few scenes are wont to do in these sublime regions. The Round, unlike its neighbors, seems a solid mass of granite, reflecting shine and shadow like a giant's face—its deep-cut features rounding off in the melting distance in well-nigh perfect symmetry, tho' rough and inaccessible to the approaching adventurous climber.

It is Bald Mountain, with scalped elephant back, that swings off to the north; and of its opposite neighbor I either **never** heard, **or** do **not remember**, the name. But **what are** names, especially **when** given by some squad of roughs or, at best, by unrealizing and perhaps religionless American surveyors? What are names to whosoever feels fit to name what moves the conceptive powers to take in, at a glance, characteristics of a talking nature? The whiter Snowy Range closes up the higher sky midway to the zenith; and a row of successions of varied mountain fronts and faces stand in motionless ranks, Nature's Sphinxes keeping Nature's Secrets, yet speaking without tongues.

The hamlet of Grand Lake, with one crane-gut street and on a sand level behind a shaggy foothill, is flanked by a brawling torrent that subsides into a placidly murmuring creek as it nears the lake it helps to feed. It has behind its back-most houses yet again a rugged ridge walling in a stretch of mountain meadow, miles square. Its new, yellow-pine houses are unpainted. Some of its inhabitants are of the rougher class, a few celebrating a grand

"drunk" periodically. The better citizens are beginning to frown down ruffianism to some effect. No
house of worship is yet erected; in fact the village is
but an infant, one however that will take some religious spanking to train it to a model youth. Rev.
Wm. Howlett, of Central City, was to visit, and did
visit, this and the scattered spots of the whole Middle
and North Park settlements; was however so unfortunate as to be blocked in by the snow, falling when
we left. He wrote me it was good I had not waited
for him, as he had been forced to return home, away
around by Wyoming Territory!

Two Weeks' Adventures.

September 12*th*.—To sum up our doings and hap-
penings, we have had rare luck. fishing—our catch
for the fortnight amounting to three bites and one
sardine four inches long! while fishermen by profession go out of days and nights—the latter often-
est—and "box" a cool seventy-five or one hundred
trout, large and small. Hunting, we have shot
eleven grouse, six beautiful teal with blue and
gold and green-gold wings, eight or ten hares and
squirrels.

There are two or three frame boarding houses on
the lake and at the village, and two of log. One of
the latter is pretty substantial and roomy, and with
a brave show of boats and sails in its miniature bays
over the outlet. The other remains unfinished, and
with partitions between apartments that partition
nothing, each occupant being allowed the luxury of
feeding ear and eye on all the sights and sounds on
his level.

Our host and hostess, rejoicing in the name of
Adams, are old Illinoisans, and quite hospitable, for
reasonable cash. Their table is of the best. Freshest trout, good beef, better venison, canned fruits
and vegetables, served with some modicum of skill
and maximum of good grace and the best of will,
are commendable rations for ten dollars a week—
and fifty cents off for every meal or night you miss.
Curious to relate, we had fresh vegetables too betimes, brought out at great expense by traveling
hucksters from Denver, who ply their trade in and
out all the settlements in the parks, but make cus-
tomers pay for the luxury to the tune of five or six
cents a pound for all vegetables and fruits they buy.
Housekeepers pay ten and twelve dollars per barrel
for flour, and fifty cents a hundred for hauling groceries and supplies, unless by special contract. Our
daily plan—of course, after invoking the protection
of God by his saints and our angels from the dangers we might meet—was to breakfast heartily and
early as possible, sling our guns and game-bags with
lunch for midday on our shoulders, tramp over flats
and mountains all day, and come back for our rel-
ished supper at 7 or 7½ o'clock, almost dark. We
met with no astounding adventures, but heard of
marvelous escapes, bear and deer hunts, without any
definite limit.

One day in Soda Creek bottom we came across
a mother with three little children, living in the
long absence of her husband in a cabin with floor
and roof of dirt, miles away from any human help
or habitation. Her sole protection consisted in two
dogs of very ordinary size, and seemingly cowards

from the way they cringed and slunk away at a
harsh word, but one full and the other a half-blooded
bull dog. Between whiles, as we were waiting for
her to boil us a little coffee to wash down our cold
lunch, the brave young mother related to us how her
two canines had had a two hours' ugly tussle with
an ancient grizzly, making the woods and hillsides
ring with the fierce roars and yells, barks and growls
of the furious contest. She had listened with bated
breath—she did not say she took any particular
means of defending the cabin — only fearful her
precious "bulls" would be torn to pieces by the bear.
Her fears were not allayed by the length of the fight
and the frequent yelps of pain and rage. The brave
little fellows came off with their lives, tho' minus
sundry paws' full of hair. And their scalping was
accompanied by smart incisions from the beast's
great claws. The poor brutes looked considerably
short of rations too—we had to drive them off half a
dozen times during our dinner—and they were as
ugly, especially the female, as the Miltonic dogs at
Hell's Gate—if not so huge.

The "Rococo" and Ptarmigan.

Anent hunting stories, I must not forget some
capital things our Louisvillian, Mr. John Barbee,
used to get up, literally, to regale our fancies, while
a frequent and most welcome guest at Mrs. Adam's
well-supplied board. He is well built, tho' more
athletic than stout, wears his miner's and hunter's
canvas rig with the manly port which is so becoming; his hair is clipped close and a pair of rimless
pebbles make his brilliant, fine blue-grey eyes more

brilliant still; while his incessant fund of humor, re-
partee, puns, inventions, kept us all enamored of his
company. One of his stories was in this sort: "The
rococo!—ho! never heard of the beast? You poor
ignorant outsiders! Perhaps you don't believe it?
Why, you know of the ptarmigan, that double-plum-
aged timber-line grouse? It is as gray as a rock, as
green as moss, and you can hardly distinguish it
from the ground where it crouches."

"Oh, yes, **of** course!" answers the addressed, a
young student, versed in books rather than in life,
and with capacity for astonishing stories probably
invented.

"Well, that ptarmigan changes color completely in
winter, so that it's white as snow and you couldn't
tell it if it were two yards from you."

"That's so, too; I've read of that and been told the
facts frequently," I chimed in.

"Yes, but that's got nothing to do with the rococo.
You know, young man"—addressing our student,
and ourselves over his shoulder—"this mountain fox
has a regular 'round' like your hunting fox. When
chased, he goes 'round and 'round a mountain top.
And mind you, he's got the right kind of legs for the
business—they're some inches shorter on the one
side than on the other so that he can run on the slant
of a hill with perfect facility, on account of the
adaptability of his limbs to his mode of locomotion.
And—"

"Oh—o! Mr. Barbee, that's a little too strong," ex-
postulated some two or three.

"Too strong, thunder! Wasn't I just now telling
you of the timber-line grouse? Is it any more won-

derful than that?   And, as I was going on to say,
you have to know this peculiarity of the fox—the
famous rococo—in order to hunt him successfully.
For, he can't run up or down—he'd tumble over—
couldn't run on a level; he'd be lop-sided and nabbed
in no time.   Then he's got to run just 'round and
'round; and all you're obliged to do is merely to
find his exact circle—let him . . —him run 'round to
where you want to catch him and just put your
hand down, with gloves on, and lift him."

"Ha! ha! that's a good one," was roared from all
sides of the table, while Mr. Barbee would compla-
cently wipe his mouth and call for "some more of
that trout—venison: you all fairly spoil my appetite."

He got our student in a corner one day and fairly
persuaded him, judging from symptoms, the rather
imaginative youth had been retailing that he was in
danger of some malignant disease: "'Pon my word,
I believe you've got it, and you'd better set in doc-
toring at once."

The patient was badly worked up all that night
and thought he discovered more and more striking
proofs of his having the disease, for certain—while
he was as lusty a young fellow as you could well
meet with just out of school.

Ice-cold Ducking.

We had a fair chance of testing some of our enter-
tainer's relations of the mountain, and found him so
truthful in some cases that we doubted whether he
was not in earnest oftener than we believed.   We
had been told of the almost natural impossibility of
catching a cold in the parks, and, one famous day,

were indulged with the fairest opportunities of
"catching our death." Coming to a series of creeks
and shallow rivers there was nothing for it but to
pull off, strip up our pants and wade—in the ice-
coldest water that runs. It failed to make us scream
with sheer pain only because we meditated upon
how unmanly it would be. We only halloed and
danced—rubbing our limbs when we got over. But
then, once or twice we attempted crossing on great
causeways of granite bowlders, so rounded off that
our hob-nailed boots slipped frequently, and, at last,
we got a considerable wetting. But the climax
came the third time, when to avoid a long road we
wanted to ford the south fork of the Grand—a
brawling half-torrent, with loose rock bed and swift
current. My more youthful companion first attempted the venture and made it with the mishap of
wetting his pants and boots. Ha! I could do better
than that. I calculated, planned—saw a clear route
and with trousers tucked high, carefully set out—
making a way about half across, when I tried to rest
my feet on some stones I had spotted from the shore;
and my misfortune began with my missteps. I
slipped on one pesky, slimy thing and trying to
balance and get on a better one, stumbled and sat
down fairly in the liquid ice. Ugh! but up and try
again. Another stumble, a lunge. the water was
sweeping me and again I nearly went headlong,
only I went the other way long. Laughter could
hardly mend things—I was soaked—gun, bag, boots,
pants, vest to halfway under my arms. And to think
of straggling home, wet as a rat, cold as an ice-house
filler, clothes flapping at every step. Fortunate for

us that we had to walk so long and briskly home.
It was our salvation—only,

"Most unkindest cut of all,"

we took nothing home besides our soaked selves but
one solitary mountain squirrel, netting about as much
meat as your moderate thumb hams, or good frog
legs.   But not the slightest cold did we catch.

Grand Lake, September 13*th.*—Last night and yesterday it was raw—raining with hail below, and
evidently snowing above, whitening Snowy Range
royally.   The bald and wooded heads above us and
below the Snowy Range are sprinkled this morning
as if with the grey hairs of old age.   It is time for
us to take warning and be gone.   As we start away
from the hostelry, the clouds are lowering on the
face of Round Mountain and the V—their filmy
trails nearly sweeping the lake shores.   It is a veil
worthy of the Grand.   We see our last of the sublime panorama fronting the outlet of Grand River.
We shall row no more over the dark blue waters—
halloo no more to the quadruple Echo, seated on the
base of the stupendous cliffs, in comparison to which
Rhenish Lorelei is but a mole-hill—and we shall
receive back no more such flute-like trumpetings as
angels might hearken to.   *Mirabilis Deus in altis!*
    We glide into a cloud-hanging mist, finally pre-
cipitating into fine rain, and drizzle, drizzle, is the
tune all the way to miserable Ostrander's—a place
I detested.   Glad to get in and warm—but our dinner was of the meanest as usual here; fried bacon
swimming in its own fat, sooted hominy—all topped
off with some compost of an apple dumpling.   Hard

eggs we got by special and repeated order, and we eked out on our appetites, some platters of schmeer-kase and the apple—what-do-call-it? To make bad worse, our driver (Mills) had a brilliant case of obstinate stomach complaint, and was as sour and uncompromising as an ancient Persian monarch about getting away, heedless of driving rain, now mixing with slushy hail and snow. But our side of the corporation, mindful of No. 1, and determined to protect ourselves, swiftly packed a lot of straw in the end of the wagon, appropriated two blankets, spread the tarpaulins over the raised spring seat in a sort of low-tent fashion, and snugly ensconced ourselves thereunder—prone but snug and defiant of mud and storm. Thus we weathered out the blowing snow storm that began to rage around us when but a few rods from the house. Blow! snow! bump! smash! scrape! trot! thump! roll!—up and down, right and left, we were hauled with only a cautious peep out on our coigne of vantage at the furious elements. After their rage was nearly spent, we could enjoy more leisurely the sight of the beautifully snow-drifted and deep-sprinkled hills, with the totally covered white summits of the range beyond, and the misty, impenetrable clouds, half-discovering, half-concealing, the lower foot-hills and the second range below the rocky peaks which closed up the sky. We resumed our shelter and fairly emerged from our manufactured bed-booth only when the wagon pulled up at Cozen's fine ranche, where we found a house full of fresh arrivals, caught like ourselves in the storm.

Frazer, September 14th.—As we start out to return over the **Range, snow covers** the whole route, scenting and refreshing the **air all the way** back to Empire. Georgetown has all **its higher elevations** white—the lower besprinkled **nearly all the way** down; and the atmosphere is **the** opposite of what we left here over a fortnight since. It is bracing, withal. Regretfully I leave—fearful lest **my** first visit may be **my** last; and such is man's life!

Georgetown, September 15*th.*—The mountains appear grander as we wing down past their suddenly projecting, and as suddenly retreating, faces—save now and anon, when longer stretches in the **circuit-**ous torrent-track afford the glorious perspective, shadowed on one, reflecting the white light on the other, side of the double panorama. The sun, midway in the western heavens, is already setting *for us,* walled in on two, sometimes on all, points of the **compass, by** the precipitous thousands of feet of God's masonry. How the

... "King of day ... rejoicing in the West,"

glares hotly thro' the narrow Canon, and dazzles the daring eye "searching his glory!"

As we bid farewell to Clear Creek Canon, **we** are treated to a gorgeous, jeweled sunset at **the** City of Golden, which stretches on either side of **the** stream in beautiful lines between the encompassing ramparts. As the reappearing sun gilds and burns the massy clouds over the mountain heads in **the west,** the fair full **moon rises** over the rock-castled ridges on the east.

The palisade rocks, **further** on, stand **out** defined and regular in the twilight. Far down beyond the mouth of the **Canon** greens the fertile, watered valley, with its corn-bearing uplands and its boshy, feathery willow low lands. The smoke alone of man's furnaces, smelting **gold, obscures** the scene of beauty and makes one sigh for the primeval untamedness of this mountain haunt of grandeur and softness of **feature** combined—like God's justice and mercy. **As we look** back, Nature's fortifications stretch in mile-wide wings with jutting buttresses to guard the passages of the hills of **God**. To the right, the shadowy, pale blue masses cut the **sky** in nobly varying lines, and great peaks loom over them in the far off.

Denver Exposition, 1883.

Denver, September 16th.—The only items jotted from the vaunted Denver Exposition—which, like bad wine, needed much praise—were: a fossil **tree** from Wyoming—a section of the trunk with open **hollow and** pillared on a pedestal, full of bright, perfect **cry**stals; some others lengthwise, and lying like a fairy cradle bedded with crystalizations; also a fine show-case full of specimens furnished by the Union Pacific Railroad Company; among which some bright red and dull purple crystals in quartz and **agate;** a cross section of the "Big Tree" from Pueblo, which is estimated at 380 years of age and measured twenty-eight feet round and seventy-nine **feet** high.

Singularly enough, *Virginia*—the State—was represented in tobacco, ores, coals, etc., from along the **line of the** Richmond **Railroad.** In the fruit department, a luxuriance of pears, peaches, and especially luscious purple and white grapes from California— **specimens** of the like in the county departments of

Colorado and New Mexico—were of fine quality.
Colorado wants to claim the finest grade of wheat
grown anywhere. Except for the expert and con-
noisseur of jewels in the rough, in precious ores and
useful metals, the Exposition is a flat affair; it is
only praiseworthy, lefthandedly, because it procured
us travelers cheap round-tickets.

But better than even its gold and precious stones
was the grandest embossed shield of the actual
moon, appearing above the horizon as we passed
into the open air, in the largest magnified disk I
ever saw—framing on her broad bosom a living section of landscape. As she diminishes in size she
increases in silveriness beyond the skill of human
artificer, as she ascends her nightly throne.

In the West, oh! what glory above and behind
the unusually dark line of the Rockies. The clouds
form in irregular bars and parallel burnings, brighter
and brighter, from the rose-red of the mists on the
left and away up on the right, to the glow of the
whitest molten gold and most fiery topaz and chrys-
olith. Just above the verge of the mountain line is
a uniform sea of the heavenliest mingling of color
which I can find no name for—it is light glorified
and glory transfigured, light of light created—the
threshold of heaven!

Land of gold, silver and jewels, Colorado Eldo-
rado! this is thy fit parting greeting. With all thy
beauty and magnificence united and blindingly
dazzling in this focused representation of all thy
wealth and worth, God give thee to be richer in
virtue and rival thy sister republic of New Mexico,
in pressing to thy rocky bosom proportionately more
Catholics than any State in the Union!

Pencilings of the Rocky Mountains.

We close the Six Weeks in the Rockies with these pen portraits from our accommodating "Nym Crinkle," as he quits the plains and reaches the sight of the dim distant mountain land.

Striking Colorado he pictures, sure enough, some greasy, rugged, slouch-hatted, or sombrero-capped Mexicans; portrays "Old Times on the Borders," in "Rice's Ranche," a solid-walled enclosure, with a flat-roofed dwelling and a bastioned tower, flanked on either hand by a park and tree rows; "New Times on the Borders," in South Pueblo, an outskirt of which shows the broad avenue, with shaded alleys, and the trim new frames, such as one sees everywhere in towns West; a life-like illustration of a "Middle Park" pasture such as we have described, not forgetting the contrast in the foot-hills:

"Behind they saw the snow-cloud tossed
  By many an icy horn:
Before, warm valleys wood embossed
  And green with vines and corn."

Our dear "Grace Greenwood," the writer's cottage at Manitou, sweet with embosking shrubbery, brawling mountain brook, crossed by rustic bridge, is struck off to the life.

Of the "Garden of the Gods" where are Poe's

Bottomless vales . . . . . .
And chasms and caves and Titan woods
With forms that no man can discover,

we have no space to speak, but can refer the curious reader to the original "Iron Trail," and the Rev. Prof. Zahm, of Notre Dame's late lectures on these very themes and illustrated with the very prints.

We may add what **Mr.** Wheeler testifies as to the health-restoring qualities of the mountain air and exercise—extending the endorsement, however, to most parts of the Rockies inhabited:

"Now as for salubriousness, I made a special study of it in Colorado, and I interviewed all the scientific men I met. The conclusion is this: Colorado, for weak lungs, bronchitis, rheumatism, **gout** and those diseases that have their origin in malaria, is a certain **cure.** It is the only place in the world where a man can get along comfortably with one lung so long as he has got two legs. All forms of phthisis are bene-fited by the air. This is not a random statement; I make it from actual experience. The dry, electric air of such places as Manitou, to say nothing of the effects of the waters, has made it the resort of invalids."

PRAIRIE DIARY RESUMED.

BLAIR, NEBRASKA, September 20th, 1883.

THE country from Omaha north to Blair, Neb., is well occupied and cultivated to a degree beyond expectation, as to the portions used for agriculture. It is, for the most part, utilized as pasture and meadow, hay being harvested in enormous quantities; and fine herds of cattle and sheep, from hundreds up to thousands, browse in the undulating hills. The surface is, however, leveler than further on towards Hubbard, where the Omaha Indians have just vacated a magnificent tract of rolling, well-watered farm and pasture lands, amounting to 50,000 acres. All this is only awaiting the United States' Commissioner's proclamation to be thrown open to expectants who will instantly take up every square rod of it. The towns, before we reach this ex-reservation and after we pass it, are flourishing and a fair proportion of them large; tho' north of Hubbard we strike again the Missouri River bottoms, thinly populated and taken up with haying operations on the usual gigantic scale.

Persons conversant with this special region say, that between the malaria and the overflows, these great wides are undesirable for anything beyond seasonable haying. The few houses we saw were heavily marked by water and mud lines high up

over the windows and under the "boxing." The
Iowa side north of Sioux City resembles this region
closely—in fact is but a continuation of it on the
opposite banks of the river Vermillion.

Avoca, Minn., September 22d.—Fulda is just now
the center of interest, the two most prominent
Bishops connected with the Colonization Society,
Rt. Rev. Dr. Spalding, President, and Rt. Rev. Jno.
Ireland, having come to give a business push to the
county, before they proceed to the spiritual object of
their visit to the Convent at Avoca, and to dedicate
the finished Church of Currie. Fulda is sustaining
its reputation and going ahead with solid strides.
More of the twin lake shores is being laid out in
building lots on ground sold by the two Bishops on
easy terms. The upper lake, contiguous to town,
has been named Lake Ireland, the lower, Lake
Spalding. About five acres on the extreme end of
the former has been sold, this morning, for $30 per
acre, to the town clerk. A new $3,000 public school
is nearly completed.

There is a practical project on hand to extend
another railroad north and south thro' Fulda and
Avoca, and taking in the vicinity of Currie and Mr.
Jno. Sweetman's large purchase. This will open out
the superb Des Moines River country and connect
with Tracy.

The surveyors are already on the route, and will
reach Murray County in a few days. The thing is
put down as a certainty by the people, and will be
of immense advantage as giving direct connections

North, and opening up the coal fields of Iowa to the prairie inhabitants, whose fuel is such a large item of expense.

CURRIE CHURCH DEDICATION.

This 23d September is the date of the long-looked-for dedication of Currie Church, built at the sole expense of the munificent gentleman, Jno. Sweetman. It is an elegant building, commodious and finely appointed, from the superb bell in the front to the carved altar in the sanctuary. The priest's residence is nearly finished and matches well with the church. The ceremonies of dedication brought the whole surrounding country to witness the grand pageant—grand for these parts—two Rt. Rev. Prelates, assisted by a number of priests, performing the sacred rites, after the public dinner furnished for all the world in the town hall. The reverent crowd of the faithful formed the living crown of the church to be dedicated as God's House—symbolical, as they girded the walls, of their own future exaltation, when they are taken up to build the walls of the Celestial Church. How appropriate the Chorister's magnificent hymn of the ecclesiastical service:

CELESTIS URBS JERUSALEM.

"Celestial city, Jerusalem!
    Of peace the vision blest,
  That high of living stones are built
    To heaven's starry crest:
  In sponsal rite art belted round
  By thousand—thousand angels crowned!
  O thou in happy lot espoused,
  With Father's glory dowered;

O Queen, most lovely of the fair
By Spouse's grace o'ershowered,
With Christ the prince in wedlock joining—
City with heavenly brilliance shining!
Here sparkling gemmed with precious stones
  Stand wide to all, the portals;
For clothed in virtue's Godly deeds
  Are thither led, e'en mortals,
Whom passionate with Christ's true love
Nor torments, nor e'en death can move.
  By pruning chisel's saving strokes,
  And smoothing touches oft
Of mason's mallet, the polished stones
  Build all the pile aloft;
And shaped with goodly joints aright
Are raised to crown the building's hight."

Ten Days at Buffalo Lake.

September 24th.—In a stay of ten days at the residence of Mr. John Sweetman—the farm villa of Buffalo Lake—it is needless to comment on the informal hospitality one receives and the home-like feeling that is cultivated in a few days' converse with the managing director of the Irish Colonization Company. Leaving aside the confidential pleasures of indoors, our journal proceeds to record that we younger folk passed most of our time on the prairie at our prescribed sports. To-day's luck sums up the bagging of some ten ducks and chickens—four ducks lost in the sloughs, and a good deal of ammunition wasted in shooting holes in the air. However, we will keep the table in game, and interchange our fine English-cooked roasts with dressed duck, chickens and smaller fry.

September 25th.—Learning we could get a trained

setter from an old hunter of the vicinity, we sped
over in haste to secure him. But bother! either thro'
our own fault or his wildness—we put it on the latter,
of course—we had a chance to lose half a dozen
chickens, and "dropped" one only.

September 26th.—Mr. Walter Sweetman accompanied us on the hunt over the rolling hills and
sloughy valleys of the farm, and great exercise did
we enjoy in the free, glorious air. If the "stillness
of the desert fill the fierce Arab with rapturous enjoyment," as Cardinal Newman writes in his "North-
man Character," how much more could we delight
in the unrestrained liberty of our blossoming prairies!
The feeling of glorious independence from the tram-
mels of fashion and "society" often makes us shout
aloud for sheer joy, thanking the great God for these
fenceless wilds, where there are no bounds but the
horizon around and the sweet skies above. The
grand thinker, Chateaubriand, joins with the strong
poet, in his "Bride of Abydos," in seeming to limit
this indescribable rapture to the nomad of the Sa-
hara; but they, like Ruskin, had something to learn
about our grand prairies. Besides this singular sensation, however, we scarcely got to-day enough
game for our sharpened appetites—a brace compris-
ing one water and one land bird, with four ducks lost.

September 27th.—Again, however, we have had
what we call another good day, securing ten pieces—
one chicken out of several flocks. People not *au
fait* in hunting, like ourselves, will count this great
luck, and professional nimrods will turn up their
noses and give expression to their contempt of such
trifling by a boisterous guffaw. Let them!

MURRAY COUNTY FAIR.

Currie, September 28th.—To-day, raw and un-promising as it is, we have had our County Fair at the pro-county seat of Murray. In default of an official report, I can say that two priests of us made ourselves conspicuous by handling vegetables and products of all kinds, weighing and measuring by the inch, yard and hour. It was a really creditable display. We have said: "This is the land of roots, *par excellence*," and here is palpable proof we were not hardly doing justice to the various and enormous productions of this soil.

Pumpkins! but let us not mention such monstrosities! Squashes! Reader, you never saw the picture of such squashes. The beets and rutabagas, Norwegian turnip, and other turnips were as big as a child could carry. Potatoes, any variety! Size: from eight or ten ounces to two and one-half pounds apiece. Cabbage? But away with such! Peas, beans; corn, green yet, and succulent for roasting ears. We had all the figures down, but it boots little to trumpet what talks for itself. One lady relates she had received nineteen premiums on as many kinds of vegetables. Outside were, of course, the horses, cattle, sheep, chickens, turkeys, wild geese tamed, etc. All stood fair.

September 29th.—Eight ducks and a brace of prairie chickens rewarded to-day's labors by land and water, somewhat counterbalancing matters, tho', by tossing a $30 rifle overboard on reaching for the last fowl.

September 30th.—Seven more ducks to-day.

HERDS AND GRASSES.

But from ducks to cattle is not as much a change of subject here, at this season, as in other parts. Farmers of considerable means do not farm so much as graze and rear cattle. It is the same in southern agricultural districts among men who have made enough by hard knocks to lie back on their oars and rest while their beeves and hogs are fattening, and coining good trade-dollars. Of hogs, of course, there are comparatively few here, but much more attention and care are spent upon cattle and sheep. Where prairies are limitless, your herds and flocks can roam at their sweet will. But it is troublesome and expensive in other respects, and you must provide for enclosures of some sort, meadows, corrals. But again, the prairie grass will not stand the constant grazing and trampling under which tame grasses will survive. Hereupon comes a question, sprung this morning, on observing that the meadow on the hillside and near the residence of Mr. Sweetman was wearing out, and on being told he had sowed tame grass over this and similar spots.

Nature has to be aided and supplemented in this matter as in the other of timber planting. It may be in place to extract somewhat from Prof. Thomson, of Nebraska's observations on

TAME GRASSES IN THE WEST,

as pertinent here: "In the prairie regions of the great West, for some time after the country is settled, only native grasses are needed. The conditions of a settled country are not congenial to the wild grasses. As a rule, tame grasses furnish feed about a month

earlier in the spring, and the same length of time
later in autumn, than the wild grasses. When the
wild grasses begin to dry up in the fall they are
tougher than tame grasses with the exception of
the buffalo and bunch grasses of the arid region
along the eastern slope of the Rocky Mountains.
There is no kind of forage which will fatten cattle
faster than our native prairie grasses during the
growing season, from the middle of May to the
middle of August."

The last statement must be modified for regions
parallel with St. Paul, and not further south than
Yankton, by pushing the latter date into September
at least, if not also in putting forward, ordinarily, the
former to perhaps the end of May. The subsequent
advice about making tame hay will not apply to
these parts, and hence to the valleys of Western
Montana, for many years to come:

"Tame hay is more nutritious, but stock usually
like good prairie hay better. Tame hay must be
made at a season when rains are frequent; while the
best time to make prairie hay is in the month of
August and the early part of September, when, as a
rule, but little if any rain may be expected."

Whereon we refer the interested reader to observations scattered thro' our summer journal. " . . . In
the latter part of the growing season tame grasses
furnish a better quality of feed than the wild sorts.

"The first and simplest mode is to sow tame grass
seed, especially timothy and blue grass, on the native
prairie, when it first begins to fall from tramping or
too close feeding. This seeding should, if possible,
be done early in the spring, on one of the late snows.

If the soil, when soft, be well scarified with a sharp harrow, it will increase the chances of a catch. With good seed sown in this way, success is almost certain.

"The only kinds of tame grasses that have been extensively tested west of the Missouri, are: Timothy, Kentucky blue grass, and orchard grass. Only red clover and white clover have been grown on a scale sufficiently extensive to justify absolute confidence. . . . ."

October 1*st.*—Mr. Sweetman brings in some ninety-three quarts of cream for the creamery at Slayton. This or nearly as much is the daily output of forty-odd cows, which yield about $1,500 a year in this way. His two hundred head of cattle and some eight or ten horses are fed in winter with the four hundred and fifty or four hundred and seventy-five tons of hay put up—except the milk cows, which receive extra feed. The triple stables are immense, and capable of comfortably housing all the live stock. A large wind-mill supplies water from a well for house, creamery and stables. Some six or seven men run the farm and stock. Cattle from Buffalo Lake are going to market only next year—the third— for cattle calved here in the year 1881.

October 2*d,* 3*d and* 4*th.*—At night we have been having heavy frosts, the thermometer ranging from 38 to 25 degrees above zero. Ice formed several nights in a hard scale on watery puddles, even on the slough shores. Snow is reported this week from St. Paul, Mankato and Sleepy Eye. Some fog and droppy rain out of the mist to-day constitute the weather record.

FALL CROP REPORTS.

Without official inquiries or figures, I learn from
private sources of farmers here and about, that wheat
has ranged in yield from thirteen to thirty-one bushels per acre, the average being somewhere about
twenty or twenty-odd for this and the adjoining
region. Oats run from forty to sixty bushels—one
poor fellow next door to us having the latter, and
almost everybody exceeding the former. Flax runs
variously from twelve or thirteen to eighteen bushels,
and sells for from one dollar to one dollar and five
cents. Oats brings only fifteen cents; wheat about
eighty cents. The corn yield has been light. Frost
has caught considerable in flat lands in the lower
levels. In general, treeless prairie corn can scarcely
be accounted except for fall feed. Vegetables, however, are just the reverse. They grow enormous,
with careful culture; and good, with almost next to
none. Large quantities of fine potatoes, fine cucum-
bers, onions, beets, turnips and beans, tolerable cabbage and parsnips, have been gotten out of this patch
of ground—second time ploughed—just over the road
from the priest's house. And I can aver it has all
not received the cultivation that would re-yield seed
elsewhere. Here are some samples from our neighboring county, Nobles. Tho' but newspaper reports,
they coincide so closely with personal observations
that they may be received with but few "grains of
salt:"

"Garret Fagin threshed sixteen bushels of flax,
twenty of wheat and fifty of oats per acre. James
Carey threshed fifteen bushels of flax, eighteen of
wheat and fifty of oats per acre. Dick O'Hearn

threshed eighteen **bushels of wheat, twelve** of flax and fifty of oats per acre."

"Mr. **William** Harrison has been threshing some. His wheat **turns out about** twenty bushels per acre, and his oats fifty. Sam. Harrison had one piece of wheat that **went** thirty-one bushels per acre."

"Tom Burke threshed thirteen bushels of flax to the acre. Tom Fagin threshed twelve bushels of flax, twenty bushels of wheat, twenty-one bushels of barley. Tim Larkin threshed thirteen bushels of flax, forty-seven bushels of oats, eighteen bushels of wheat to the acre. Mr. **R.** O'Day has been threshing **on** the Boyle farm, north of town, and gives the following results: From **seventy** acres of wheat they got **1,400** bushels; one hundred acres of rye, 375 bushels; **nine** acres timothy, seventy-seven bushels, and flax 478 bushels, or fifteen and one-half bushels to the acre."

From Pipestone **County Fair** we have this general **corn** record:

"Considering the season, corn of astonishing size and **in** great abundance was displayed. Ears from twelve to fourteen inches long and proportionately large **in** circumference, and stalks ten to twelve feet high, do not grow every year in every county, but such were on exhibition at the Fair."

J. T. Suffron's exhibit **of** pumpkins: "On less than an **acre** of ground planted promiscuously thro' the **corn,** he has raised one hundred and seventy, a large **majority** of **them perfectly ripe,** and many of them **extra** large size, three of which weighed respectively **forty-six** and one-half, sixty-two and one-half and **seventy** pounds. The two largest **were** purchased on sight by the enterprising Close Brothers, to be placed on the tables in their office for exhibition, to show what Pipestone soil can produce."

From Jackson County: "Reports and big samples continue to roll into the 'Republic' office of the immense and perfect crop of potatoes raised in Jackson County this year. We last week spoke of a citizen of Jackson raising one and one-half bushels of white elephant from two potatoes, and now in comes Mr. Gillis and scoops the Jacksonite by raising a plump two bushels of the same kind from the same amount of seed. And Barney Quinn, the jovial settler up the river, from the Emerald Isle—he has raised some 'whoppers' of the star variety, and reports getting an honest ten bushels of the raspberry variety from twelve seed potatoes. H. S. Schlott, of this village, has grown large quantities of several new and choice imported grades."

Finally from Murray—our own county—we present these:

Thos. Doolin threshed six acres of wheat that yielded thirty and one-half bushels per acre, and four acres of flax which went twenty-eight bushels clean.

Mr. H. Stanley's threshing machine, run by Wm. McDermet, threshed seven hundred and ten bushels of oats for H. Scovell, of Cameron, from morning until 10 o'clock.

Only one, A. B. Smith, raises 1,270 bushels of oats on eighteen acres, or seventy-one bushels per acre! which is hard to swallow.

October 7th—Sunday.—At leisure from the busy flurry of the moilful week, we can rest on the Lord's day, aye, and Lady's day, the solemnity of the sweet Holy Rosary. To-day is blowy and rainful, fitfully. Heavy summer rain, and distant thunder prevailed last night, and the low, soft, white mountains in the East, that looked earth-mountains of snowy piling, had melted into the leaden rain sky, until just now, when the sun, struggling with the watery vapors, gave signs of conquering. Autumn and Summer are contending too, and suggest the descriptive lay:

PRAIRIE OCTOBER.

God give unbosomed Summer
  Yet awhile to stay:
Nor muffled Winter cumber
  Prairie sky and way!

To-day is lowering, leaden—
  Mournful pipes the breeze;
Blades yellow, leaflets redden
  —Fall hath painted these.

But yesterday was blooming,
  Softly warm the clouds!
Ah me! the Winter's looming,
  Fierce in snowy shrouds.

October's life November
  Chills and palsies thro':
Bleak winds blow, man, remember,
  Summer's dirge for you.

Yet hope! the sun grows whiter,
  Fleece clouds gem the blue.
—Death's life foreruns a brighter—
  Be among the few.

Sprite month, days russet—shady,
  Whose each Sunday's thine,
Conduct us, Angel's Lady,
  Thro' life's chequered shine!

October 9th.—I see reports of Indian summer visiting our neighbor counties. I believe it has come in its northern guise to our **Avoca**. The three past days have been warmer; in fact, quite warm at times. Even the nights have been a trifle close until frost accompanied the clear evenings. Soft clouds and warm tinted sunrises and sets have brought geniality. The birds twitter some again. I don't find the sweet haziness, but seldom at least—that is a characteristic of lower latitudes. The equableness is disturbed by fretful gusts of storms and wind. The weather changed perceptibly yesterday evening from what it was in the morning. At first, before noon, out footing after a stray flock of ducks or chickens, I got into a great lather of perspiration, well madefied thro' and bathed. Riding in the afternoon, a good fall overcoat was a necessity. And so it changes.

The muskrats are building high and narrow, and I heard a shrewd farmer predict an autumnal winter, more open than usual. The muskrats know if Vennor don't.

October 10th.—Mr. Drueke, agent of a large grain firm, reports thirteen car-loads of flaxseed of four hundred and fifty to five hundred bushels each— since about a month—received and shipped from here. He paid ninety-five cents. It advanced to $1.05 here. Rumor says to $1.17 in Fulda. The agent expects to export some 20,000 bushels of flax from here by January 1st. Up to last Saturday Avoca had shipped twice as much seed as Fulda; and only Hadley, twelve miles above, had reported more. Wonderful. tho' natural, to relate, only thirty bushels of wheat have left here; people only raising for their own consumption. One Thos. Hargedon says he has housed one hundred and fifty bushels of wheat—some damaged—a tolerably large yield, if rightly measured.

Our Indian summer has been rudely broken into last night and this morning by a fall of snow, which melts pretty much as it touches ground. The roofs and trees were plentifully sprinkled with a light coating of white at six A. M. Our hunting for the past ten days has been sporadic, resulting in only scattered braces of duck and trios of chickens, in all about sixteen pieces, including some yellow-shank snipe. Some fine specimens of snow-white. long-billed pelicans were shot at Mr. Dan. Murphy's in the last fortnight. They had the great pouch under the bill, and were so white they were mistaken for swans on the wing. Ducks are swimming by hundreds and thousands; some seeming inclined to migrate. Geese quack about every day. Chickens even yet are found in quantities. All game is shy and hard to get at.

By 11 or 12 M., the snow has, after a more violent effort at a little blowing storm, subsided, and the evening has been of fitful sunshine. Wintry clouds hang about sullen and cold. Conquer Autumn!

Nuns' School Examinations.

October 12*th.*—In view of the superficiality and humbuggery of public school examinations of fourteen and fifteen-year-old girls for teachers—some right here, who are given certificates or offered such before their papers are examined—it is refreshing to see the semi-annual examination reports of the III

and V Forms, in the schools of higher grade of the
Nuns of the Holy Child. Here are specimen questions answered by a girl thirteen years old in her
third year: *Geography*— Draw from memory map
of Central Europe. What rivers empty into the
Baltic, North, Mediterranean. Adriatic, Black Seas,
etc.? For what are these cities remarkable, and
where situated?—Lyons, Sevres, Leyden, Tokay,
Trieste, Basle, Pisa, Lausanne, etc. (The map drawn
is excellent, fit for copy for the press. It is colored,
and the principal rivers, mountains, cities, and many
of minor importance are given, especially in France
and Germany.) *Natural Philosophy*—What is com-
pound motion? Illustrate. (And the illustrations
are real pieces of art for a child, better than most
printed ones.) Define Cohesion, Adhesion, Capil-
lary Attraction. Why do salts, etc., dissolve in
water? What is motion? What are gravitation,
gravity, weight, etc.? *General Knowledge*—What
do you know of the history of pottery? General
characteristics of a family of birds—describe? Describe process of making leather. *French*—Qu ap-
pelle-t'on verbes irreguliers? Temps simples de l'in-
dicatif, subjonctif, des verbes: *savoir, dire, courir*—
leur auxiliares? Ecrivez une lettre descriptive: Ceque
vous savez sur le riz, le clou de girofle, le cafeier, la
canne a sucre. *Latin*—Of possessives, declension,
conjugation. Translation, parsing. Nine questions.
(And these, with the ones above in French, are answered rather better than some others; the French
notably so, because of the French extraction of the
pupil.) *United States History*—Principal battles
fought in Revolutionary war: year, name, American

and British Commanders, victors, accounts of particular battles, Burgoyne's campaign, sketch of Washington's life (map is attached of American Indians,
a rather difficult subject for grown persons.) *English History:* Chart of Tudors and Stuarts, Lady J.
Grey, account of reign (?) of **Oliver** Cromwell, Ar-
mada, **Elizabeth.**

Church History—St. Paul's journey with large
map (good.) The ten persecutions, emperors, and
popes, and other martyrs. Heresies between I
and VIII centuries, Apologists, Latin and Greek
Fathers, sketch of two Saints, St. Paul of Thebes,
St. Cecilia.

Grecian History — Map of Archipelago and
Greece, and Coast of Asia.

English Literature—History of Robert of Sicily.
Explain: *meet, blare, Saturnian, reign,*
dais, clerk. Derive: *Chant, sedition,*
words.

Grammar — Parsing. What are t'
ments of **English?** Describe Greek el
what other sources are some words (
the child gives a list of four to six w(
teen different languages, at thirteen ?
report is, however, genuine withou!
abounds with faults of grammar and (
raphy, blamable much on her Frenc

THE V FORM, by a girl sixtee?
braces Astronomy, Higher Gran
Physical Geography, Physiology,
tory, etc.

I. *Astronomy*—(with tolerabl
North Polar section of the spl

memory, as those given above.) Signs of Zodiac for three months, North ecliptic constellation, *Hydra* and *Centaurus*.

II. *Grammar*—Analysis of Milton's "Sonnet on Blindness." Uses of "it." Gerund. Table of Auxiliaries: strong, weak and mixed verbs: *Do, beware, quoth, ought.* Infinitives.

·*Literature*—Shakespearean Dramatists, dates and works. Writers and Poets from Elizabeth to Restoration. Ben. Johnson, on "Decay of Drama," Lives of Cowley, Walier or Benton and Hobbes. Criticize Milton as poet and prose writer, his works, "Paradise Lost."

IV. *Geography*—Character of Ocean Currents, (fairly good and full). Explain all about them, in seven questions. Atmosphere, Winds, Monsoons, Routes, United States to Europe, Australia, Map of vicinity of New York city (more than most people know).

V. *Physiology*—Skin, Hands, Nails, Teeth, Voice, Lungs, Heart.

VI. *Mediæval History*—Eight Crusades—Table of Summary, Fred. II., Fred. Barbarossa, Emancipation of Cities, Feudalism, Chivalry, Sketch of Knight Templars. Contemporary Sovereigns of IV Epoch, with great men. Table of events and persons in V Epoch of Middle Ages, Rudolph of Hapsburg, "Golden Bull," "Hundred-years" War. Council of Constance, "Sicilian Vespers," Rise of Ottoman Empire and taking of Constantinople, 1453. Map of all.

Avoca, October 11*th.*—Record of Mr. Mike Shankey's threshing: J. Fitzsimons, one hundred and

eighteen bushels flax   Phil. Flynn, wheat, one hundred and thirty-three bushels; flax, two hundred and
fifty-one and one-half bushels; oats, four hundred
and ninety bushels. Jno. Johnson, wheat, sixty-
eight; oats, sixty-one; flax, one hundred and twenty-
five. Pat. Dwyer, over nine hundred of oats; two
hundred and thirty flax; some four hundred left to
thresh; wheat over two hundred. Pat. Farrell, oats,
seven hundred bushels. Lawrence Brien, 1,100
bushels oats from twenty-two acres; wheat, three
hundred bushels from eighteen acres; barley, two
hundred and thirty-six from nine and one-half acres;
flax, one hundred and five bushels from twelve
acres; peas, seventy-five bushels to the acre. Pete
Conroy, of Avoca, twenty-seven bushels of wheat to
the acre; fifty-two of oats; seventeen of flax; had
very tolerable corn.

PRAIRIE INDIAN SUMMER.

October 12th, 13th, 1 *th and* 15th.—Our Indian
summer has resumed its milder sway, and we are
having glorious days and fine, tho' hoar-frosty,
nights; the frost making almost as thick a layer as
the actual snow we had. Birds of hardier kind are
about yet, and I have seen several yellow and other
colored butterflies. Flies trouble one but little, still
make their presence felt. About 10 to 2 P. M., or a
little later, the sun is quite warm to the exerciser. A
hearty sweat can be had on short notice for the chase
of a chicken or duck. We have enjoyed several
sunsets, one specially fine colored and the sunrises
are, if not warm, clear and beautiful. The painting
the prairie fires, now rampant, make on the horizon

are nearly as varied as the clouds. The smoke slants
up in a rippling mass, dark pink, even crimson, betimes. The flames remind one of fiery sunset clouds,
except, of course, they change more rapidly, and lick
up into the curling smoke with their great forked
tongues.

Looking at the village to-day from off in the prairie, it has the appearance of what we enjoyed in the
young spring time, save for an undefined haziness.
Trees are fast losing their verdure, and still more
their leaves. I just learned one could buy a tolerable-
sized tree, on a district about a lake some distance off,
for seventy-five cents. Cheap fuel can be had at
Mankato for $2.50 or $3.00 per cord, the freight to
here of course extra. It is hard and good.

October 16th.—High cold wind blew from southeast nearly all day, and we have stirred out but little.
Struggling Sol was ruled out, and his fitful shine but
added gloom to the mournfully piping winds. This
is surely too cold for even Indians in summer.
The rawness effects more than the cold. We have
had several fine messes, Fridays principally, of frog-
legs. The creatures have been swarming, jumping
the lake banks in living cataracts, for these two or
three weeks, all about the prairie in several rods of
the water. They are the orthodox green and brown
edible frog, proved so by the good eating we have
got by frying and stewing them. Pity some youngsters do not get up an industry in frogs, killing them
with sticks, or better, beating them down to the lake
shores, where others could hold long nets and scoop
them up by the literal thousands. They would sell
well in any city or town of size.

October 17*th.*—The blow from Southeast turned in some rain upon us last night, and to-day it has been keeping up a steady gale of some velocity, accompanied by intermittent, driving rain and sometimes sharp showers. It was cold, even cutting, on about noon and up to dark.

October 18*th.*—The weather has changed to the opposite pole of crystal clearness, comfortable warmth in sun and with exercise, ushering in with a bright sunrise, and going out with a roseate sunset, fringed with galleons of crimson edged with fiery jewels. The night fell under one of those topazine skies, lustrous, shaded, and contrasted against blue islands— a face of a nun in her hood of white and serge. Our but little waned moon shone out in her empyrean sphere, softening all. We had a short hunt before dinner, and before supper. We got but one fine-plumaged wood duck out of two water fowls we shot, and the ones which flew away with possible loads of shot in and about their feathery coats. If a cat has nine lives, surely some drakes can boast of ten. The other day we killed a regular northwestern diver, and for want of better had it served up to some newcomers, who devoured it all in a trice, and smacked their lips over it.

TRICKS ON TRAVELERS.

This is not the first we have had cooked for connoisseurs. We put a mud hen or two on the table before some Eastern ecclesiastics, and they ate them without a whimper. Even a full-blooded John Bull averred there was nothing peculiar or distasteful about them, tho' he didn't eat more than a taste.

The worst joke we have practiced was to mix a prairie squirrel—practically a burrowing rat—before an eminent dignitary on the same platter with a rabbit or hare.   He ate several quarters of it without changing countenance.   And yet here comes an English-bred and nourished gentleman, who uses profane expressions when you mention eating frog-legs to him!   We'll serve him some for dinner to-day in a stew or fry, and wager he'll eat and drink without nausea, sucking frogs' toes!

Some one characterizes "a Scotchman as one who is never at home except when he is abroad;" an Englishman, "one who is never contented save when he is grumbling;" an Irishman as "an individual con-tradictory, who is never at peace unless he is fight-ing."   *Bon-mot*, not far from the truth.   I believe—I know—English *eat* too much, not to speak of drinking; "thinking they should starve," as a gentle-man just over and well acquainted with their habits, says, "if they didn't eat five meals a day—at least four square ones.   At 9 A. M. a great, solid break-fast; lunch big as an ordinary meal, only cold (and who would not lunch on English cold beef roast?), at meridian; dinner proper at 4 P. M., and with tea at six; a gross supper between 9 and 10 P. M.   To this may be added a *tasse de cafe*, when they awake in the morning, if they do before regular breakfast time.   It is rather discouraging on sacerdotal spirit-uality to learn these five meals are the *mot d'ordre* in an English seminary."

I fancy it will be rather a disadvantageous change, if not an impossibility in the line of mortification, for those accustomed to five or even four dainty meals, to come down to two rough repasts on something as strong as corned beef or *uncorned* pork and sourkraut, as is so often the practice here in winter. People naturally staying up late and rising not much before nine or ten o'clock in the morning, in the short cold days of only about half the length of the summer days—eight or nine hours—it would be folly to eat more than say two regular meals and a luncheon. One finds, however, his appetite calls for the substantial, and he can stow away so much at a sitting that he will not be considered safe in replenishing too soon.

October 19th.—Our capture of frogs this morning was a splendid failure, as the cold, biting winds drove the poor leapers into their hiding places. Of the millions generally seen hopping around we found but a few benumbed little stragglers, not worth attention as game, and too pitiable to touch.

The northern breezes have played havoc with our Indian summer again, and nearly stripped the remaining leaves, already

" . . . Fallen into yellow . . . . and sere."

This fits pre-eminently the description of the greater grasses; nothing apparently remaining green but scattered bunches of blades on the sides of the new breaks. Last night a skim of ice from one-half to three-fourths of an inch coated the small sloughs, and the water left over in buckets and barrels froze an inch thicker still. It was some warmer at and after noon, turning again bitterly cold towards sunset, heavily beclouded. I begin to believe the ducks and geese are migrating or proximately preparing to move South. They fly about violently and rest-

lessly, higher than usual. Messengers **seem** scurry-
ing back and forth, bent on business communications
requiring dispatch. Flocks are growing larger, and
crowd into greater masses. There are no vegetable
islands on upper Lake St. Rose, as we had last fall.
On these used to congregate the flocks of smaller
and greater snipe, and tiny water birds; and however ungenerous it may seem, we took advantage of
the innocence of the creatures, and, rowing up,
poured broadsides into them that soon filled a good
pail with the choicest game. Our once carefully
rigged, flatbottom sail-boat is lying up at "Arbor
Point" in a dilapidated condition—the hulk under
water, the rudder broken, mast loosened at the base,
and sail flapping. How I could tweak the nose of
that opposite and obstinate Norseman who took the
"sail" to get home, and tied it so carelessly the gale
broke it loose and drifted it here to **ruin**.

I heard to-day of a farmer who has two dozen
hogs he has fattened on unripe corn and is ready to
sell. Others might imitate this *scheme.*

Flax has advanced to $1.07 at Avoca, and $1.12 at
Fulda; tho' raisers say they would rather sell here,
five cents a bushel not paying for hauling further.

October 21*st.*—We predicted snow last night; and
to be sure, we peep out this morning and **see** the
ground covered to the depth of several **inches** and
flakes still falling. The wind is from the southeast,
and it is not distressingly cold, in fact much more
pleasant than yesterday or the day before, overhead,
tho' the roads became very muddy this afternoon.
The snow held up about 10 A. M., and melted
nearly all away by night, day setting cold and
drizzly.

I have heard of and seen nothing in the shape of
game, except some whitebodied, quacking geese,
flurrying west.

October 23*d*.—Tho' the snow disappeared from
Avoca and thereabouts on the 21st, it remained at
Woodstock, thirty miles above, till last night; also
on the road to St. Paul. I find it lies pretty thick at
and about Kasota and all along the line to the Mississippi. It is something like an ordinary snow in
Kentucky, half-and-half snow and sunshine, little
falling and melting soon.

EASTERN AND WESTERN "VALLEY OF THE IM-MACULATE."

October 27*th*—30*th*.—As we pass thro' Southern
and Eastern Wisconsin the short meadows are green,
like choice plots about the wooded region of Minnesota. Some fine, tho' less frequent, lakes diversify
the landscape, framing their mirror-bosoms in the
rustic copses of the shores. We leave the rugged
pineries and dalles and cataracts far towards the
North and West, and glide over wooded prairies
now.

MADISON, WISCONSIN.

I do not find the corn better, in many places, than
on the Minnesota "*Coteaux des prairies*" we have
just left, until we approach the border country between Wisconsin and Illinois. Here the staple
grain seems, from the specimens we spy in passing,
about of a similar quality and quantity per acre as
on the wooded portions across the valley of the "Immaculate Conception"—the old Catholic name for
the Upper Mississippi. It will bear still further re-

petition, that the southeastern part of Wisconsin is very like its compeer's corresponding portions across the river in singular beauty and fertility.

An Irish gentleman farmer has gone so far as to compare feature for feature of the soil, natural growth, *land-lie*, etc., of Southeastern Iowa with the best agricultural regions of the interior of England. Similarly, one might counterpart rural Belgium, the inland Rhine provinces, Alsace—any of the best and most picturesque prairie portions of Europe—in a random selection from the better lands in the prairie belt west of the Mississippi—in the country watered by the still greater Missouri and its tributaries—the Platte, Niobrara, James or Dakota. There are simply no finer—scarcely as fine—lands in the wide world, as can be selected here by a mediocre judge. But it speaks for itself, this eastern valley of the "Immaculate Conception," as we will persist in calling it, in spite of the seemingly hopeless fixing of the Indian-derived, but doubly corrupted name.

Mississippi is neither the right Indian appellation, nor the original one given its waters by the pioneers, Hennepin, Marquette, LaSalle, LeSueur and their comrades. It takes observation to determine that, in fact, the Missouri is the "big" as well as the "Muddy Waters;" and that the Mississippi, of entirely different character, is but its greatest northern tributary. This tributary is vindicated as the original discovery of the priests who named it for its amber-like limpidity, its green shores, and sweet islands, its now and again expanding lakes, as the river of the "Immaculate."

CATHOLIC FUTURE OF THE AMERICAN PRAIRIES.

Shall this omen, this constant tradition, be buried with the bones of the only half-immortalized Recollect, Hennepin — the but lately recognized Marquette? It behooves Catholics of Europe and **America**—above all English-speaking Catholics—to continue to answer this galling question by joining in the increasing chorus from Catholic throats, that are making the "Immaculate Conception Valley" ring with the acclaim: "Blest Mary shall be dowered anew with these beautiful **and** broad lands of hers, in bountiful compensation for the loss of her dowry in once Catholic England and Europe." Catholics shall so "possess the land" by the meek conquest of occupation and immigration into the western valley of the Mississippi, that every State and Territory in its imperial extent shall rejoice in an ever-expanding majority of the children of God and Blessed Mary Immaculate.*

It is being done—the Church is extending her borders and widening her tent, more beautiful than the painted skins of Solomon's, in Minnesota and Iowa, Dakota and Montana, Nebraska and Kansas, Arkansas and Missouri, on to the Rocky Mountain States and Territories. Nay, we leap the grand Rockies and extend her glorious bounds from the "great river even unto the sea." Balboa, who feasted his eyes on the Pacific, but represents feebly the mighty multitude of Catholics who shall one day make the sea alone the boundary of the sweet conquests of the Mother of Civilization, the only Church of the living God.

---

* This practical **work of the** Colonization Association will be much advanced by the **Rev. J. J. Riordan** at his post in **Castle** Garden, New York.

Nor will it be by mere rhapsodies—tho' enthusiasm be the great prime mover of all great designs. Take the square of about a dozen States and Territories from the British to the southern line of Kentucky. Missouri, and westward to the Rocky Mountains, including, however, New Mexico. Bound its western limit by the Rockies and the east by the two greater lakes and the Indiana eastern boundary. And in this area of about 22 degrees, respectively, of latitude and longitude, you have in the valley of the Upper Mississippi, in this year of grace 1884, over 2,000,000 Catholics, under four Archbishops, with eighteen suffragan Bishops and Vicars Apostolic, and two Coadjutors. These twenty-four Prelates are assisted by 2,600, near 2,700 priests, who serve 3,200 to 3,300 churches and chapels.

The schools of all grades, from the theological seminaries to the humble orphanages, number upwards of 1,500, with 177,000 students and pupils, taught by over 4,400 religious and lay teachers. Most of these figures are only approximations—estimates more or less accurate, but not calculated to mislead into exaggeration.

Continually inflowing tens of thousands up to hundreds of thousands of immigrants from abroad, and of migrators from the South and East, make accuracy almost impossible, but allow additions instead of subtractions.

It needs no extraordinary talent of forecast to predict what is being actually fulfilled before our eyes, that these dozen States, by the first decade of the twentieth century, will have swelled to sixteen or eighteen and sustain twelve, or at least ten millions

more of people—near half of whom *shall* be children of the Church. The Apostolic Vicariates will
have grown to Bishoprics—Bishoprics to Metropol-
itan Sees. Kentucky, or more probably Indiana, on
the east of the valley may compete with Minnesota
or Nebraska on the west, for the next Archiepiscopal Sees. Many new Sees are bound to follow the
great influx of Catholics on all the prairie lands to
the very roots of the Rockies and from Montana to
Mexico, in proportion as the center of the whole
population moves steadily and rapidly from the
middle of the Ohio Valley towards the juncture of
the Mississippi and Missouri Rivers. Our most
Catholic cities on or near the Atlantic, the great
Lakes and the Mississippi. are made the largest of
the Union by their millions of Catholics, who con-
sequently have not room to turn round in their tene-
ments or in their churches. And these cities must
give up their wanting poor and starving souls to
freedom and plenty and salvation on the boundless
prairies of God. The overcrowded, and conse-
quently ill-served churches of the North Atlantic
States must, perforce, send their surplus Catholics
West, if they would save them from temporal and
spiritual loss—not to say, damnation. There must
come a crash if the eastern and western pans of the
scales be not more equally trimmed. The West possesses what the East desires — room and feed.
Happy shall be the lot of the Church in her new
conquests and gatherings of her multifarious children, if she but find ever the same zealous coadjutors
to build up homes and altars for her dear ones!
That she shall be equal to the task we have proof

in the unprecedented increase of dioceses and arch-
dioceses in Wisconsin, Michigan and Illinois. See
the corresponding increase of the Church's priests
and people, crowding the shores of all the lakes of
our northern line. Look across the Mississippi and
see whether you do not recognize the new Chicagos,
Milwaukees and Clevelands rising in the new West.
Illinois and its northern neighbors do not much more
than compete with the opposing States over the
valley in temporals or spirituals. The child will soon
be the equal of the parent—the State of yesterday
with the State of the day before yesterday.

Twenty-five miles north of Chicago you have but
a model of what the environs of St. Paul and Minneapolis and the twin cities of the Mississippi and
the Missouri will become in a quarter of a century,
more or less.

The Twin City of the Upper Mississippi is already
third in expenditure of wealth and increase of buildings in the Union—either one of the pair, seventh in
the long list of American cities.

God bless! Mary extend her white hands over,
these consecrated regions; give increase of the earth
as it retards not in the road to heaven, and make
this the chosen home of as many devoted millions
as failing Europe, our crowded East and poorer
South, can pour on the prairies!

CONCLUSION.

But there is another aspect of the comparison of the Eastern as put alongside the Western Valley of the Mississippi. It is the business aspect of finding better locations for homes, more room for farms, better farms—the many advantages of the West over the East, as a region to people with those specially having no good establishment where they are and possessing moderate means to start elsewhere. As to the persons themselves, no one is going to be so mad in this practical community of ours as to advocate wholesale, indiscriminate exoduses of the poorer and better-to-do classes, of malcontents, really solid farmers, tradesmen—everybody to make up at once a Commonwealth complete. Selections (percentage) are all the East needs to give, and all the West cares to have, to make both better off.

One by one, or at least, the society unit, family by family, is the oldest and best style for civilized people to emigrate and migrate, unless such peculiar circumstances—such unbearable hardships of life, of Government or community hatred should make it reasonable for many to leave together and settle down again together.

The Horace Greeleyan advice has some pith of wisdom in it. But he said cautiously, "I say—"as if afraid of his too great generality of invitation, even after being restricted to the "young man" class. If it was only relatively good then, it is less good now. The isolation and separation of sexes will cause as much dearth of women in the prairies as of men in the manufacturing districts of New England.

The West wants indeed, at first, agriculturists—practical farmers, and more of them than she possesses. Still, it is not such an anomaly to invite more city people, tradesmen, mechanics, and those who have no such settled occupation, to join with farmers and mingle among them, learn from them and become like them. Farming is easier West than East of the Mississippi, and our inventive genius has made knowledge common and once exclusive experience the boon of the community. Nature favors machinery more in the West, and the unpracticed can learn to run machines where they would be long awkward at manual labor at the plough, hoe, axe-handle. Besides, too many youngsters have crowded the cities, and are trying to shirk labor by seeking clerkships, and find both spiritual and temporal loss in the midst of unaccustomed contaminations. Fifteen years ago it was proven that the very great majority of those living in the country principally east of the Mississippi, were crowded, into about fifty cities. What is this but the country people wresting themselves from their legitimate occupations and usurping the places of townpeople? The balance must be restored by giving back these crowded millions to their God-given and once possessed freedom—health, home, faith—by transferring them back to their *native* occupations. It is only trimming the scales by restoration of equal weights, of accustomed weights.

The rural population ought to exceed the urban—
the country at large to contain much more than often
badly-selected sites to crowd millions into and crush
the life and energy out of them, make machines of
them for selfish purposes, for monopoly, for the
glutted few — the aristocrats among us who are
becoming nobles too fast, and have too many vas-
sals. We want no oligarchies, and we shall go on
creating them, or bolstering up still more the ones
already in power, and disposed to use their power,
even against the will of Legislatures and Senates?
We want Catholics especially to be freed from tram-
mels and vassalage, filth and consequent endemics
and epidemics, elbowing and discontent. We want
broader fields for their ambition, greater aims for
their designs, better and farther-reaching results
from their hard labors. The ground faces of the
poor must be uplifted and look abroad on plenty;
the worked-down must have some content of life,
and not curse the day in which they were born. A
time will come after the communities in the West
grow larger and more comprehensive of all that is necessary for a good civil life and temporal prosperity,
when we can invite with more confidence the poorer,
the worse-provided classes of our brethren to sit
down at the board of plenty in the household of
faith built up in the glorious West. We do now re-
strict invitations to those who are not perhaps suf-
fering worst in the built-up and overcrowded cities,
simply because the poorest are shiftless when thrown
entirely on their own resources, and would not only
suffer more, probably, when left to make a subsistence
on the prairies than in the city, but would be a burden

on those who are not uncharitable so much as they are unable to stretch their hands in relief, for a few years, beyond their own thresholds, and have to feed the mouths more dependent upon them.

But the time of the poorer shall come, and it shall come the more quickly by those just above them leaving the poorer their places by moving West, and giving the same a chance to rise to some industry, self-dependence and energy of practical work before they expose themselves to the hardships they would not survive. Where, next, ought people to come from inside our United States, and to what spots ought they to migrate to furnish those prairies of ours with their proportion of population and render them the granary of the world? No man can specify where they should not come from, provided always the individual families are not well established and have means to move. Not to be too general, however, a letter of August, 1880, (private, but tacitly left free to publish) from Rt. Rev. John L. Spalding, of Peoria, opens both sides of the practical questions by determining as follows: "Nebraska and Dakota are the best points in the United States for settlers. Several new railroads are building into Dakota, and homesteads of 160 acres can be had very near the depots. There is a great rush for these lands, and our good Kentucky Catholics will wait until they are all gone. Dakota has a fine climate and excellent soil. There are Catholic settlements in Kentucky where the soil was never good and is now worthless." * * * These predictions have been fulfilled, and the choice shown good. Since the middle of '80 the efforts of the

Colonization Associations have been directed successfully to the obtaining of lands for Catholic settlements in one of these two regions, and the many
others south to the Gulf, commented on twice or
thrice in these pages. The recent wise appointment
of Rev. J. J. Riordan, of St. Peter's, N. Y., now at
his self-sacrificing post at Castle Garden, will speed
the practical working of the settlements, both for
immigrants and migrators in the West. I have
heard the colonization authorities often assert that
the railroad lands in Minnesota have about all, if not
quite all, been taken up, and you can now, outside
the general offers of the colony agents, only watch
your chances for obtaining choice spots from the
scattered dissatisfied or the non-Catholics in the
vicinity of Catholic settlements, who want to sell
out and go farther. The other States and territories
have plenty of room for fine selections, to please all
tastes and judgments—from the very warm to the
much colder climates, and with soil of almost the
identical formation in all our latitudes.

The prospector ought to look for and inspect the
desiderated locations for himself and those intimately
interested; for, good and less good, tolerable and
proximately useless lie side by side, in these as in all
other farming and grazing sections. And when
he shall have definitely chosen, he may congratulate
or blame himself first and last, and not be necessitated to fall back on vituperation or praise of those
from whom he has obtained general or particular invitations. No one knows exactly what may fit another in land any more than he can judge precisely
what will fit another in a hat.

Finally, as to where to move from?

The episcopal remark about the thinness and the present uselessness of certain regions in Kentucky can be verified to the letter. The State has so long been settled and picked over, tho' sparsely populated and never invitingly opened to immigrants, that the great majority of farming sections have already gotten into the hands of tight-grip owners who will not part with their holdings under a high consideration.

A large section of the Bluegrass region was once largely in the hands of Catholics—and now, in the district of Georgetown and White Sulphur, for instance, but from three to five names of the old Catholic settlers can be found opposite these magnificent lands in the assessor's books.

About Lebanon in Marion, Bardstown in Nelson, Springfield in Washington, many well-to-do Catholics of the old Maryland stock are scattered among many more non-Catholics; and great portions of the country are rocky or worn, and contain nothing like what ought to be, by this time, the thousands of children of the original sixty families of the famous league of emigrants from St. Mary's. and the shores of the Chesapeake, and descendants of later comers. The older settlers, again, in Breckinridge and lower Daviess Counties are comparatively comfortable in comparison with their fathers, but have yet to grub in only tolerably productive soil for their now-accounted short crops of corn and tobacco. Breckinridge, especially, the old "Bracks in the Ridges," is true to its name, and is rather more inclined to mountainous than hilly. The newer settlers among Catholics have gotten poor lands, and wear out their fingers' ends moiling in the rugged ridges and the rougher forests for often but a bare subsistence. Who would blame many from wishing to better their condition by migration?

Our Ohio River-bottom farms, on both shores, are among our most valuable for grain production, but have so often, of late years, been subject to overflows, that they invite cultivation by their richness, and repel by the manifold chances of seeing the farm produce, cattle, houses and all swept down to the Mississippi. Besides, except in Union and the borders of Daviess and Henderson Counties, the better locations are not possessed by or salable to other than wealthy Catholics.

Those indeed of our Kentucky farmers who have moved to Missouri on the bottoms of the Mississippi have not fared much better, being often ruined by disastrous overflows as frequent as ours. As to Illinois and Indiana the inference is obvious that their Ohio river boundary lands, of very much the same fertility as the opposing Kentucky shores, are the victims of the same watery destroyer, tho' no one disputes the safer fertility of back-lying farms. A great —perhaps the greatest—corn and railroad State is the "country of the Illinois;" but it is so surrounded and run over by water in its lower lying portions, and even on the flatter prairies, that it takes considerable expense to make its prolific soil yield its full complement. One who has traveled much in, for instance, the belt between Watseka on the east and Hennepin on the west, after thanking God, turns to congratulate man on the invention of the ubiquitous, ever-crossing and re-crossing railroads—they are nearly the only mode of locomotion in parts of the year.

Lower middle Indiana, to judge from what one can see from repeated transits by rail, seems productive enough as far north as Indianapolis; but the higher in latitude you ascend the more unpopulated— if not depopulated—the prospect appears; and the land seems to yield little beyond scrub-oak and sparse weeds, until you touch the counties bordering on Michigan. Thousands have moved from these, and the Indiana and Wisconsin prairies on west. No one who has traveled along the boundary lines of Illinois and Indiana can speak well of what he can see from the trains. It is one of the most uninteresting and apparently hopeless regions on the whole prairie east of the "Great Waters" for farming purposes. Michigan will scarcely come into our count; Wisconsin farms, tho', may, and stand fair in comparison of either their western or southern neighbors—at least in the parts south from a line drawn from the St. Croix river opposite St. Paul to a point above Milwaukee.

Most of these States, indeed, have other and for them much more profitable outlooks in their coals, timber and minerals, as Kentucky and Michigan; in their manufactories and pineries as, respectively, Wisconsin and Illinois. But it may be said broadly that none of them will finally yield the same riches in grain and general pasturing, and must turn to riches of another source before they will, in the long run, compare favorably with the "Golden West."

FINIS.

CONTENTS.

DEDICATED TO OUR LADY IMMACULATE.

www.ingramcontent.com/pod-product-compliance
Lightning Source LLC
Chambersburg PA
CBHW030327270326
41926CB00010B/1535